A History of the Cronulla Sharks

Fourth Edition (2023)

Matthew Geddes

First published in Australia in 2017 by
Parallel Partners
PO Box 190
Crookwell NSW 2583

Geddes, Matthew

A History of the Cronulla Sharks
ISBN 978-1-68419-026-3

Cover Stars: Club legends Greg Pierce and Steve Rogers hold the Amco Cup trophy, 1979.

Produced by Parallel Partners Books

Introduction

When the New South Rugby League commenced competition in 1908, the area south of Sydney known as Cronulla had just acquired its name. The area had been subdivided in 1895, but it wasn't until 1911 that steam trains connected the seaside village to the Sutherland-Illawarra rail line.

In 1932 the Cronulla-Caringbah Junior Rugby League club was established. The club's A Grade side was invited into the Sydney premiership's second division in 1963.

In 1967, the NSWRL invited teams from Penrith and Cronulla to join their expanding competition to reflect the geographical sprawl of Sydney. The new team from the shire was known as Cronulla-Sutherland.

The Sharks, as they are known, moved to Endeavour Field midway through the 1968 season. They are the only club to own their own ground. Endeavour was one of the first grounds to have naming rights when it was sponsored by Ronson in 1985. It has since been known as Caltex Field, Toyota Park, Remondis Stadium, and as of 2016, Southern Cross Group Stadium. It has also been known simply as Shark Park.

Cronulla benefited from the relaxation of transfer rules in the NSWRL in the early 1970s. The signings of tough English international players Tommy Bishop and Cliff Watson helped the club to become a premiership threat.

Locals such as Steve Rogers and Greg Pierce became international superstars, and joined players such as Paul Khan, Steve Kneen and the Sorensen brothers from New Zealand, Dane and Kurt, to keep Cronulla a competition heavyweight into the early 1980s.

The Sharks dabbled in Super League in the mid-1990s, and have been a regular visitor to the end of season finals games over the last two decades.

As of 2016, a new crop of promising players were becoming some of the next superstars of the game. Players such as Jack Bird and Valentine Holmes joined hardened veterans Paul Gallen, Michael Ennis and Chris Heighington to produce the longest winning streak in the club's fifty year history; and ultimately, their inaugural premiership success.

It all started back at the Sports Ground in April 1967, under the coaching of the legendary Australian test hooker Ken Kearney.

1967

Former Australian Ken Kearney had already spent more than a decade as a first grade coach before joining Cronulla for their first season in 1967. A captain-coach of Australia's 1956 Kangaroos Squad, Kearney had also been instrumental in the early years of St George's record eleven premiership wins in a row. He spent three years at Parramatta in the early 1960s, and transformed them from easy beats to finalists.

Kearney brought former St George prop Monty Porter to a Sharks side that was made up mostly of locals. Balmain centre Dave Cooper and five-eighth Jack Danzey joined the club for their first year, as did St George lower grader Warren Ryan, and Wentworthville halfback Terry Hughes.

Cronulla played their first match in April 1967, against Easts at the Sports Ground. Easts had gone the entire 1966 season without a win, but had a new coach in Jack Gibson. Both sides scored one try, and four goals from Terry Hughes gave Cronulla an 11-5 win to celebrate their elevation to the top tier in style. John Hynes was the club's first try scorer.

In round two, Cronulla soon realised how tough the competition was when they were beaten 30-12 by 1966 runners up Balmain at Leichhardt Oval.

Hughes kicked six goals against Souths in round three, but it wasn't enough to prevent a 23-15 defeat at Redfern Oval.

Round four saw Cronulla play in front of their home crowd for the first time. At Sutherland Oval, the Sharks scored three tries to one on their way to beating Parramatta 23-11.

A 19-7 loss to Wests was followed by a 29-15 defeat at the hands of top of the table Canterbury. When Cronulla were trounced 29-9 by Newtown in round seven, only fellow newcomers Penrith were below them on the table.

In round eight, Manly winger Les Hanigan scored a club record five tries, as the Sea Eagles thrashed Cronulla 39-5 in the first match of what would become a long standing rivalry.

Cronulla fell to the bottom of the table with a 20-9 loss to premiers St George, before two tries from Monty Porter and five goals from Terry Hughes set up a 19-13 home win against North Sydney.

In the first meeting between the newest members of the competition, Cronulla went down 13-10 to Penrith at Sutherland. The Sharks were in last place at the halfway mark of their inaugural season.

By round twelve, Easts, under Gibson, had become a finals hopeful; and were too strong for Cronulla, running out winners by 11-4.

A hard fought 6-6 draw with Balmain saw Cronulla rise above Penrith and Parramatta at the bottom of the table.

The Sharks conceded five tries in a 29-14 home loss to South Sydney, and were back at the bottom after going down 15-10 to Parramatta in round fifteen.

The next week, Cronulla were thrashed 26-0 by Wests. The heavy losses followed, as the realities of a long season started to hit home. The Sharks were beaten 25-6 by Canterbury, 22-9 by Newtown and 27-7 by Manly to be three points behind the rest of the field with three games to play.

A 42-6 mauling at the hands of St George in round twenty, and a 30-6 thrashing from Norths confirmed Cronulla would end their first season with the wooden spoon.

Cronulla ended the year with a 22-5 away loss to Penrith. The Sharks finished five points behind the Panthers in last spot.

Terry Hughes was far and away the top scorer for the club in their first season, with 139. Monty Porter and Dennis Hewett were the club's leading try scorers with just three apiece.

Cronulla had lost seventeen of their last eighteen games in a tough debut season. Kearney stayed on as coach, determined to lift the club away from the cellar.

1968

Cronulla signed former Wests hooker Noel Thornton and Central Coast five-eighth John Monie for 1968, in an attempt to bolster their attack.

The club started on the right track, upsetting 1967 runners up Canterbury 16-12 in the opening round of the season. Both sides scored two tries, but the goal kicking of Terry Hughes proved the difference.

Hughes scored two tries as Cronulla went down by 22-13 to Norths in round two. A tough 8-6 loss to Parramatta, and an 18-11 defeat from Easts saw Cronulla slump to eighth place.

In round five, Cronulla fought hard against premiers South Sydney, but went down 15-9 at Redfern Oval, thanks to three field goals from Rabbitohs' fullback Eric Simms.

The Sharks conceded five tries in a 29-15 loss to St George, before sneaking home 16-13 against Balmain at Sutherland Oval.

Four goals from Terry Hughes got Cronulla home 13-12 against Wests in round eight, despite the Magpies scoring two tries to one.

In round nine, Hughes was again the hero; kicking five goals and a field goal in an 18-17 win over Newtown at Henson Park. It was the first time Cronulla had strung together three wins in a row.

The winning streak came to an end when the Sharks went down 13-7 to Manly. An 18-8 loss to Penrith saw Cronulla turn the midway point of the season in tenth place.

A 32-4 thumping from Canterbury followed, before the Sharks played their first game at their new home of Endeavour Field. In June 1968, in front of a crowd of just over 8,000; Cronulla beat Parramatta 10-7.

Cronulla went down 14-9 to Easts before being thumped 32-9 by Souths. Brian James and Ron Coote both scored doubles for the Rabbitohs.

Cronulla pushed St George all the way before going down 23-18 at Endeavour in round seventeen. They were no match for Balmain the next week, falling 23-7 at Leichhardt.

After a 19-12 away loss to Wests, Cronulla had their best win of the season in round twenty. John Monie scored a club record four tries as the Sharks ran in eight on their way to a 36-11 thumping of Newtown at Endeavour.

It was to be their last win of the season. Cronulla went down 32-5 to Manly and 17-6 to Penrith, to finish the season in tenth place; ahead of Norths and Newtown.

Terry Hughes was the club's top point scorer with 167. Hughes was also named the winner of the inaugural Rothmans Medal for being the best and fairest player in the competition. He was also the Sharks' leading try scorer with seven, one ahead of John Monie.

Hughes was soon to get a new scrum base partner in the form of tough as teak St Helens halfback, Tommy Bishop.

1969

Apart from the key signing of Tommy Bishop, Ken Kearney strengthened Cronulla with the acquisition of Queensland and Australian test hooker Noel Gallagher, and former Newtown international forward Graham Wilson.

Centres Paul Taylor and Ray Corcoran became regular first graders, and enjoyed the service of the new halves combination of Hughes and Bishop. Second row forward John Maguire also became a key player for the Sharks. Local junior fullback Greg Pierce made his first grade debut in 1969.

Despite the recruitment drive, Cronulla conceded five tries in the opening round 21-10 loss to Norths at Endeavour Field.

The Sharks were soundly beaten 25-7 by Balmain before being crushed 43-4 by premiers Souths at Redfern. Mike Cleary and Denis Pittard each scored three tries for the Rabbitohs in a result which left Cronulla languishing at the bottom of the ladder.

Cronulla went down 29-19 to Easts, before letting in seven tries in a 35-15 away loss to Penrith. An away 17-8 loss to Manly left the Sharks winless after six rounds.

Cronulla conceded eight tries in a 42-15 loss to Canterbury. Berries forward George Taylforth scored 24 points.

The Sharks finally broke through for a win in round eight. Noel Thornton scored a hat trick as Cronulla beat fellow strugglers Newtown 30-14 at Henson Park.

Cronulla were unlucky to go down 11-10 to Wests the next week; and then fought hard in a 19-12 loss to Parramatta. The Sharks dropped back to last spot at the halfway mark of the season after going down 16-12 to St George in round eleven.

In round twelve, John Maguire scored two tries as Cronulla upset Norths 19-12 at North Sydney Oval. They followed up with an 18-15 loss to Balmain and a tough 8-3 loss to Souths.

In round fifteen, Cronulla scored four tries to three against Easts, but went down 21-16 to remain stuck in last place. They went some way in their attempt to avoid the wooden spoon with an 11-8 win over Penrith the next week, with Tommy Bishop scoring the only try of the match.

Cronulla went down 15-8 to Manly, and 28-17 to Canterbury, before beating Newtown for a second time, 26-15; scoring six tries in the process.

A 20-10 loss to Wests ensured Wests finished 1969 with the wooden spoon for the second year in a row. They finished their season with a 22-14 win over Parramatta at Cumberland, and an 18-12 home loss to St George.

Ken Kearney resigned as coach at the end of 1969. Tommy Bishop was appointed captain-coach for the following season.

For the third consecutive season, Terry Hughes finished the year as Cronulla's leading point scorer, with 80; ahead of Gordon Abercrombie on 52.

Young centre Paul Taylor was the Sharks' top try scorer with seven, one ahead of rookie second row forward John Maguire.

1970

After scoring 24 points for Canterbury in a match against Cronulla in 1969, George Taylforth joined the Sharks for the 1970 season. He was joined by a number of rookies, including hooker Ron Turner, lock forward Chris Wellman, centre Bob Wear, and five-eighth Kevin Hogan, who eventually replaced Terry Hughes. After a disappointing 1970 season, the former Rothmans Medal winner Hughes returned to Wentworthville to finish his career.

Cronulla started life under the leadership of Tommy Bishop with a 23-13 win over Newtown in the opening round of the 1970 season. Both sides scored three tries, but seven goals from George Taylforth enhanced the margin for the Sharks.

The Sharks were unlucky to go down 18-17 to Canterbury at Belmore in round two. They scored three tries to two, but a field goal from Wayne Peckham secured the win for the Berries.

Cronulla were belted 33-14 by Easts in round three, and then went down 24-11 to premiers Balmain. A 15-13 loss to St George in round five saw the Sharks slip towards the bottom of the ladder.

Cronulla went down 21-12 to Norths, 21-10 to Manly, and 17-15 to Wests before upsetting 1969 runners up Souths by 25-6 in round nine. The Sharks scored five tries to two in the win.

The Sharks were beaten 27-16 by Penrith, before six goals from George Taylforth helped Cronulla beat Parramatta 18-9 in round eleven. At the halfway mark of the season, Cronulla sat in ninth spot, well short of the top four.

In round twelve, Cronulla scored five tries to two, and Taylforth kicked eight goals in a 33-12 victory over Newtown at the Sports Ground.

The Sharks followed up with a tough 11-2 home win over Canterbury. Ray Corcoran scored the only try of the match.

A 17-13 loss to top four side Easts was followed by a shock 33-9 win over Balmain in round fifteen. Cronulla had seven different try scorers in the win.

Cronulla went down 10-2 to St George, before beating Norths 19-12 at Endeavour. Unable to make the finals, but safe from the bottom of the table, the Sharks turned in uninspired performances against Manly, going down 26-14; and Wests, losing 16-2.

In round twenty, Cronulla went down 21-16 to top of the table Souths. The following week they belted Penrith 23-2; and finished the year with a 34-6 thumping of Parramatta at Cumberland Oval. Paul Taylor scored two of the Sharks' eight tries. Cronulla finished the season in seventh spot; their best ever result.

George Taylforth set a new club record of 202 points to be Cronulla's leading scorer for the season. Tommy Bishop was the club's top try scorer with nine, one ahead of Ray Corcoran.

1971

Apart from Terry Hughes returning to Wentworthville, Cronulla lost John Monie to the Newcastle competition, robbing them of valuable depth in the halves.

Newtown's goal kicking back Dave Cotter joined the club, while young halves Barry Andrews and Fred Dennehy took the most of their opportunities. Penrith lock Maurie Raper also found a new home at the Sharks in 1971.

Cronulla started the season in style, scoring eight tries in a 42-3 thrashing of Norths at Endeavour Field. Dave Cooper and Kevin Hogan each scored doubles, while George Taylforth kicked nine goals.

The Sharks followed up with a 31-12 home win over Penrith. Taylforth kicked another eight goals, while hooker Ron Turner crossed for two tries.

In round three, the Sharks went down 16-15 to 1970 premiers South Sydney. A 10-9 loss to Newtown and a 23-17 loss to Easts saw Cronulla drop out of the top four at the end of round five.

In round six, Cronulla went down 24-20 to St George in the match of the day at the Sydney Cricket Ground. Tommy Bishop scored two tries for the Sharks.

Cronulla returned to form with a 22-6 win over Wests in round seven. Kevin Hogan scored two of their four tries.

In round eight, Cronulla produced a major upset; beating competition leaders and 1970 runners up Manly 7-0. Rookie Peter O'Brien scored the only try of the match.

Cronulla were smashed 35-12 by Balmain, before going down 20-11 to Parramatta, and 28-12 to Canterbury, to be in eighth spot at the halfway point of the season.

The goal kicking of George Taylforth helped Cronulla to a 17-16 win over Norths, despite the Bears scoring four tries to three.

A 9-5 loss to Penrith, and an exciting 21-20 defeat at the hands of Souths proved Cronulla were competitive, but still lacked the firepower to become a premiership threat. Young five-eighth Barry Andrews scored a try and six goals against the Rabbitohs.

In round fifteen, Ray Corcoran scored a hat trick as Cronulla smashed Newtown 25-2. They lost 11-7 to Easts before upsetting St George 19-15 at Kogarah. Dave Cotter scored three tries in the Sharks' first ever win over the Dragons.

Bob Wear and Ray Corcoran each scored two tries as Cronulla defeated Wests 22-13 at Lidcombe Oval in round eighteen.

A 22-7 loss to Manly ended any slim chances Cronulla had of making the finals. The Sharks went down 9-7 to Balmain before beating Parramatta by 15-9 at Endeavour.

Cronulla finished their season with a dour 9-3 home win against Canterbury. The finished the year in seventh spot.

Dave Cotter was Cronulla's leading point scorer in 1971 with 78, ahead of George Taylforth on 57 and Ray Corcoran on 51. Corcoran scored all his points from 17 tries, which was far and away the best for the club. It was also equal second best in the competition alongside South Sydney's Bob McCarthy. They fell one short of Balmain winger Paul Cross.

Tommy Bishop decided he needed to bolster Cronulla's forward pack if they were ever going to truly challenge for the finals. He looked homewards to Great Britain for a solution, but found another one on his doorstep at St George.

1972

Tommy Bishop knew he had a potent enough backline at the Sharks, especially after the try scoring prowess of Ray Corcoran in 1971.

Cronulla was strengthened by the signing of two key forwards for the 1972 season. St Helens prop Cliff Watson joined the club. The Great Britain international lent an air of menace to the pack. The other key acquisition was Ken Maddison from St George. A member of the Dragons' 1971 Grand Final team, Maddison brought the experience of 100 first grade games to the Sharks forward pack.

Cronulla started the season with a four tries to three 26-13 win over North Sydney. The margin was enhanced by seven goals from Barry Andrews.

The Sharks went down 5-2 to Penrith in a forgettable match, before being crushed 37-0 by St George at Kogarah. The Dragons scored seven tries, and Graeme Langlands kicked eight goals.

John Bonham scored three tries and nineteen points as Newtown smashed Cronulla 27-12 at Endeavour in round four.

A 30-16 loss to premiers Souths was followed by an 18-12 loss to Wests. Cronulla fell to equal last spot alongside Parramatta.

In a battle for last place, Cronulla defeated Parramatta 32-18 in round seven. Bob Wear and Ray Corcoran each scored two tries.

The Sharks conceded eight tries, including four to winger Bill Mullins, as they went down 38-21 to Easts at the Sports Ground.

Cronulla went down 26-5 to Canterbury and 19-5 to Manly before beating Balmain 10-6 in round eleven. The Sharks were in tenth spot at the midway point of the season.

The Sharks went down 17-15 to Norths before sneaking home 12-10 against Penrith, thanks to a penalty goal from Barry Andrews.

A 14-13 loss to St George and a 16-14 loss to Newtown typified Cronulla's ability to compete without getting over the line. At the end of round fifteen they were still in tenth spot, with no chance of making the finals.

Chris Wellman and Paul Taylor were the try scorers in a 13-2 upset win over Souths in round sixteen. The win put a dent in the Rabbitohs' premiership defence.

Barry Andrews kicked eight goals in a 25-7 away win over Wests; and five against Parramatta as Cronulla ran in six tries in a 28-10 away win.

Cronulla went down 25-18 to Easts and 14-9 to Canterbury; before pushing competition leaders Manly all the way in a 15-10 loss at Endeavour.

The Sharks finished the 1972 season with a 34-11 win over Balmain at the Sports Ground. Fred Dennehy and Ray Corcoran each scored two of Cronulla's eight tries. The Sharks finished the season in eighth place.

Barry Andrews was Cronulla's top point scorer for the season with 151. Ray Corcoran was again their leading try scorer with thirteen.

1973

Dave Cotter left Cronulla at the end of 1972 to join Canterbury. It had become clear Cotter was not a major part of Tommy Bishop's future plans.

Young centres Steve Rogers and Eric Archer were very much a part of Cronulla's future, as were outside backs Rick Bourke, Warren Fisher and Steve Edmonds. St George prop Grahame Bowen joined the Sharks for the 1973 season, which saw the finals expanded to include the top five teams.

In the opening round, Cronulla defeated Newtown 21-18 at Endeavour. Rookie winger Steve Edmonds scored two of Cronulla's five tries.

Cronulla went down 20-17 to 1972 runners up Easts, before sneaking home 15-14 against Souths. They found their best form in round four, scoring seven tries to one in a 33-7 belting of Wests at Lidcombe. Greg Pierce, Bob Wear and Cliff Watson all crossed for two tries.

The Sharks went down 14-11 to Balmain before beating top of the table St George 12-5, to join the Dragons in second spot, one point behind Canterbury.

Cronulla dropped to fifth place after going down 11-5 to Norths, and stayed there with a tough 11-5 away win over Parramatta in round eight.

The next week, Steve Rogers scored two of Cronulla's four tries as they defeated Penrith 22-8. A 12-8 loss to premiers Manly was followed by a 24-10 win over Canterbury at the SCG in the match of the day. Rogers scored another double for the Sharks in the win which saw them in fourth place at the halfway mark of the season.

Cronulla scored four tries to one in a 16-7 win over Newtown at the SCG in round twelve, and moved into second place with a home 12-7 win against Easts the following week.

In round fourteen, Cronulla scored five tries to one in a 19-9 win over Souths at Redfern. A 20-13 win over Wests on the back of two tries from Ron Turner saw the Sharks move four points clear of third spot, but they were still three behind leaders Manly.

Eric Archer scored two of Cronulla's five tries in their 21-0 win over Balmain in round sixteen. The Sharks went down 15-10 to St George at the SCG the next week, but hung on to second spot.

Cronulla bounced back to beat Norths 20-9, thanks to doubles from Ray Corcoran and Tommy Bishop. The next week Bob Wear scored a hat trick as the Sharks ran in eight tries in a 32-3 thumping of Parramatta.

In round twenty, Greg Pierce and Bob Wear scored two tries each as Cronulla belted Penrith 32-13. Steve Rogers kicked seven goals against the Panthers.

Cronulla snuck home 9-7 against Manly in the match of the day at the SCG, before finishing the regular season with a 19-12 win over Canterbury. The Sharks finished in second spot, just one point behind minor premiers Manly.

Cronulla had qualified for the finals for the first time. They played St George in the major preliminary semi-final, and went ahead 6-0 on the back of three goals from rookie centre Steve Rogers.

Tommy Bishop scored a try shortly after half time, and a late try from former Dragon Ken Maddison secured an emphatic 18-0 win for the Sharks.

Cronulla went on to face Manly for a spot in the Grand Final. Sea Eagles' winger Max Brown crossed on the stroke of half time to give Manly a 5-2 lead.

Bob Fulton dominated the second half; scoring a try and kicking two field goals to set up a 14-4 win for Manly.

Cronulla faced a Newtown side in the final that had been forced to progress through a replay win against St George. Greg Pierce, Steve Rogers and Chris Wellman scored tries to set up a 20-11 victory which propelled Cronulla into the Grand Final for the first time.

Cronulla's side in the 1973 Grand Final was Warren Fisher, Ray Corcoran, Eric Archer, Steve Rogers, Bob Wear, Chris Wellman, Tommy Bishop (capt), Greg Pierce, John Maguire, Ken Maddison, Grahame Bowen, Ron Turner and Cliff Watson. Rick Bourke played as a reserve.

The 1973 Grand Final is remembered as the most brutal in memory. Both forward packs were hell bent on taking each other out of the game. Manly lock forward and playmaker Malcolm Reilly was taken out of the game with an injury after 25 minutes.

Referee Keith Page issued several blanket warnings, but they went unheeded, and Page's inability to send anyone from the field gave a green light to the continuing violence.

The class of Bob Fulton prevailed. He scored a try late in the second half to give Manly a 5-0 lead at the break.

Steve Rogers kicked a penalty goal to get the Sharks on the board, before Fulton scored a second try to give Manly a 10-2 lead.

Rick Bourke scored a late try for the Sharks but it wasn't enough, as Manly ran out winners 10-7 to secure their second premiership.

Steve Rogers was Cronulla's top point scorer with 119. Tommy Bishop was the club's leading try scorer with nine, one ahead of Ken Maddison and Bob Wear. Bishop resigned as captain-coach at the end of the season. His legacy will forever be leading Cronulla to their first premiership decider.

1974

Former hooker Noel Thornton took over as coach of Cronulla in 1974. The club Great Britain internationals Tommy Bishop and Cliff Watson, but signed Australian winger David Waite. Rookie centre Dave Chamberlin and prop Peter Ryan made their first grade debuts during the season.

Cronulla started the season with an uninspiring loss to Newtown. They went down 10-2 to the Jets, before being thumped 44-13 by Easts in round two. The Roosters ran in ten tries.

Two tries each from Warren Fisher and Ray Corcoran helped Cronulla to a 26-24 win over Souths in round three to get their season off the mark.

Cronulla went down 17-8 to Canterbury and 28-24 to Penrith, before being thrashed 40-5 by St George in round six. The Dragons ran in eight tries, as Cronulla slumped to second last spot.

The Sharks bounced back to beat last placed Balmain 22-15, thanks to two tries from Ken Maddison. They snuck home 11-10 against Norths the next week, before smashing Parramatta 21-0. Ray Corcoran and Eric Archer each scored doubles against the Eels.

In their first meeting since the 1973 Grand Final, Cronulla upset Manly 27-18 at Brookvale. Ray Corcoran scored two tries as the Sharks ran in seven tries to four. Cronulla went down 16-6 to Wests in round eleven, and turned the halfway mark of the competition in eighth spot, just a win short of the top five.

A dour 4-3 win over Newtown was followed by a 30-5 shellacking at the hands of Easts. Cronulla lost 22-12 to Souths and 34-8 to Canterbury, before a 14-11 defeat from Penrith all but ended their chances of making the finals.

Steve Edmonds scored a hat trick, and Chris Wellman and David Waite each crossed twice as Cronulla beat St George 31-17 at Kogarah in round seventeen. A 21-14 win over Balmain was followed by a 19-13 victory against Norths. Cronulla went down 27-10 to Parramatta before pushing premiers Manly all the way in a 21-20 loss at Endeavour. The Sea Eagles scored five tries to two, but seven goals from Barry Andrews kept the Sharks in the match.

Cronulla finished their season with a 20-8 home loss to Wests. The Sharks finished a disappointing season in tenth spot. Steve Rogers was the club's top point scorer with 52, ahead of Barry Andrews on 44. Ray Corcoran was the leading try scorer with ten.

1975

Legendary St George and Australian lock forward John Raper replaced Noel Thornton as coach of Cronulla for the 1975 season.

Prop forward Grahame Bowen retired, but Raper otherwise inherited much of the 1974 squad. Prop forward Paul Khan joined from Brisbane, while young rookies John Purcell and Greg Mullane made their debuts for the club during the season.

Cronulla started their season with a four tries to two 20-18 home loss to Penrith. Steve Rogers scored fifteen points for the Sharks.

In round two, Cronulla upset 1974 runners up Canterbury 26-15 at Belmore. They followed up with a 17-13 win over premiers Easts at the SCG.

A 21-14 loss to a resurgent Parramatta side saw Cronulla drop to fifth spot, but they kept their place with a 17-13 win over Norths on the back of four goals from Steve Rogers.

Cronulla scored four tries to two in an 18-16 win over Newtown before going down by the same scoreline to Balmain in round seven. A 12-12 draw with top of the table St George kept Cronulla in fifth spot.

The Sharks consolidated with a 41-11 thrashing of Souths. Ray Corcoran scored a club record equalling four tries as the Sharks ran in nine.

Cronulla lost 24-18 to Manly and 26-20 to Wests to turn the halfway mark of the competition in fifth place.

A 20-11 loss to Newtown in round twelve saw Cronulla fall out of the top five. The next week they conceded eight tries in a 40-15 loss to last placed Penrith.

A tough 6-4 loss to competition leaders Easts was followed by a 23-9 win over Parramatta. Dave Chamberlin scored a double against the Eels.

Warren Fisher scored two of Cronulla's four tries in their 18-5 away win over North Sydney which saw the Sharks back on the cusp of the top five.

Four goals from Steve Rogers helped Cronulla to an 11-3 win over Canterbury in round seventeen, which moved the Sharks back into the top five.

A 14-13 win over Balmain was followed by a 10-7 loss to St George. Cronulla clung to equal fifth place after going down 23-17 to last placed Souths in round twenty.

In the second last round, Cronulla went down 26-16 to Manly at Endeavour. The Sea Eagles scored four tries to two, and Graham Eadie finished with seventeen points. The loss saw Cronulla drop to seventh spot.

Cronulla ended their season with a disappointing 31-17 home loss to Wests. They finished eighth, just one win short of the top five.

Steve Rogers was Cronulla's leading point scorer for the season with 156. Dave Chamberlin was the club's top try scorer with nine, one ahead of Rogers, and centre Paul Taylor.

At the end of 1975, Cronulla again looked to England for a playmaker that could take them to the upper echelon of the competition.

1976

John Raper remained as coach of Cronulla in 1976. Ken Maddison retired, while former Australian hooker Ron Turner joined Newtown, and lock forward Chris Wellman signed with Wests.

Parramatta hooker John McMartin joined the Sharks, and was joined by Great Britain international halfback Roger Millward.

Rookie wingers Tony Graham and Martin Raftery became regular first graders, while firebrand second rower Steve Kneen also made his first grade debut for the club.

Cronulla started their season with a 27-15 home loss to Manly. A 20-20 draw with Canterbury was followed by a 15-12 loss to 1975 runners up St George.

The Sharks were belted 28-9 by Parramatta in round four, and were in last place as the only club without a win.

In round five, Cronulla broke through for their first win of the season with a 32-18 belting of North Sydney. Warren Fisher scored two of the Sharks' six tries.

Cronulla went down 22-11 to premiers Easts, before beating Penrith 28-20, with Warren Fisher again crossing for a double.

The Sharks went down 22-18 to fellow strugglers Newtown, before producing an upset 39-5 smashing of Souths. Martin Raftery scored a club record equalling four tries.

Cronulla beat Balmain 17-14, but went down 23-10 to Wests to turn the halfway mark of the season in ninth spot.

Five goals from Steve Rogers helped Cronulla sneak home 16-15 against Penrith, but they went down 20-9 to Manly the next week.

In round fourteen, Cronulla beat Canterbury 24-8 on the back of two tries from Martin Raftery and six goals from Roger Millward.

A 14-13 loss to St George cruelled Cronulla's momentum, and a 23-0 smashing at the hands of Parramatta left them in ninth spot with six rounds to play.

The Sharks bounced back to beat Norths 19-8 on the back of two tries from Warren Fisher, but were crushed 33-13 by Easts the following week.

Greg Pierce and Fred Dennehy each scored two tries as Cronulla beat Newtown 28-11 in round nineteen. A 19-16 loss to Souths the next week ended any chance of the Sharks making the finals.

Cronulla went down 11-9 to Balmain before ending their season with a 20-17 win over Wests, thanks to two tries from Eric Archer. The Sharks finished the year in eighth spot.

Steve Rogers was Cronulla's top point scorer with 74, ahead of Barry Andrews on 54. Rookie winger Martin Raftery was the club's leading try scorer with fourteen.

1977

John Raper stepped down as coach of Cronulla at the end of 1976, and was replaced by former St George five-eighth Ted Glossop.

Roger Millward returned to England, while Greg Mullane joined Canterbury and Tony Graham signed with St George.

Kiwi front rower Dane Sorensen joined the Sharks, as did Newtown halfback Steve Hansard. Rookie fullback Mick Mullane became a key player during the season.

Cronulla started the season with a tough 7-5 win over Canterbury at Belmore. Barry Andrews kicked the decisive penalty goal.

The Sharks went down 21-10 to Easts and 23-13 to Balmain, before beating Norths 12-7 to be in seventh place at the end of round four.

In round five, Dave Chamberlin scored two of Cronulla's four tries in a 22-10 win over St George. A 37-10 win over Newtown at the SCG on the back of a hat trick from Steve Edmonds, and nineteen points from Steve Rogers, saw Cronulla sneak into the top five.

Four goals from Steve Rogers gave Cronulla an 11-5 win over premiers Manly in round seven. An 18-17 win over Souths the next week saw the Sharks move up to third place.

Cronulla went down 18-17 to Penrith, 22-15 to Parramatta and 25-2 to Canterbury to drop to seventh position at the halfway point of the competition.

An 18-14 loss to Easts was followed by a 20-12 win over Balmain at Leichhardt, which kept Cronulla within a win of the top five.

In round fourteen, Cronulla beat Wests 23-12 thanks mostly to seven goals from Barry Andrews. The Sharks went down 21-15 to Norths and 15-10 to St George to be two wins short of the top five with six rounds to play.

In round seventeen, Cronulla ran in nine tries in a 45-12 annihilation of Newtown at Endeavour Field. Rick Bourke equalled the club record of four tries in a match, and Barry Andrews finished with eighteen points.

Cronulla fell further short of the top five with a tough 12-8 loss to Manly, but seventeen points from Steve Rogers helped the Sharks to a 23-9 win over Souths which kept their finals chances alive.

In round twenty, Cronulla scored nine tries as they thumped Wests 47-10 at Pratten Park. Dave Chamberlin crossed for a hat trick, and Steve Rogers scored a club record 26 points.

Dave Chamberlin scored two of Cronulla's nine tries as they beat Penrith 41-10 to be within a win of the top five with one round to play.

Seventeen points from Steve Rogers helped Cronulla to a 23-18 win over Parramatta in the last round, but it wasn't enough to secure a finals spot for the Sharks. They finished the year in sixth spot.

Steve Rogers was again Cronulla's leading point scorer with 146, ahead of Barry Andrews on 95. Rogers was the club's top try scorer with eleven, one ahead of Steve Edmonds and Dave Chamberlin.

Ted Glossop left Cronulla after one season as head coach to join Canterbury. The Sharks had the bulk of a top side, and were just in need of a premiership winning coach to fulfil their potential. That coach arrived in 1978 in the form of legendary St George and Australian second row forward, Norm Provan.

1978

Norm Provan won a record ten straight premierships as a player with St George. For the last four, he was captain-coach. Provan also took Parramatta to the finals in 1975.

Goal kicking halfback Greg Cox joined the Sharks from Balmain. Forwards Gary Stares and John Glossop became key first graders during the season.

Cronulla kicked off their season with a comfortable 25-7 win over Souths. The Sharks scored five tries to one.

Steve Rogers scored two of Cronulla's six tries in a 28-2 win over North Sydney in round two. The Sharks scored four tries to two in a 20-18 win over Parramatta at Cumberland to share the competition lead with Manly at the end of round three.

Cronulla scored three tries in a 21-4 home win over Easts, and took the outright competition lead with a 35-9 win over Penrith. Dave Chamberlin scored two of the Sharks' seven tries.

In round six, Cronulla defeated premiers St George 25-17. They scored five tries to three, and Barry Andrews finished with thirteen points.

After a tough 16-4 win over Newtown at Henson Park, Cronulla suffered their first loss of the year in round eight. The Sharks went down 14-11 to Canterbury, but remained on top of the table.

Cronulla bounced back with a 14-12 win over Balmain, but then went down 27-8 to Manly at Endeavour. A 20-2 loss to Wests saw the Sharks drop to second spot behind the Magpies at the halfway mark of the competition.

The Sharks went down 21-10 to Souths, before sneaking home 15-12 against Norths. Cronulla beat Parramatta 15-5 in round fourteen to stay within a point of Wests at the top of the table.

After going down 18-5 to Easts at the Sydney Cricket Ground, Cronulla smashed Penrith 43-4 on their home turf. The Sharks ran in nine tries, including a double to Dave Chamberlin. Steve Rogers finished the match with nineteen points.

Cronulla scored five tries to one in a 23-11 win over struggling St George at Kogarah, and returned to the top of the table after beating Newtown 44-0 in round eighteen. The Sharks scored ten tries against the Jets, including doubles to Steve Edmonds and Dane Sorensen.

Cronulla beat Canterbury 14-4, and Balmain 23-8; but lost top spot when they were again defeated by Manly, 26-4, at Brookvale Oval.

The Sharks went down 18-17 to minor premiers Wests in the final round, and finished in second place, ahead of Manly on percentages.

Manly went into the major preliminary semi-final as favourites, after comfortably beating Cronulla twice during the season. The Sea Eagles led 4-0 at halftime, but tries from Eric Archer, Mick Mullane and Steve Rogers saw Cronulla streak away in the second half. Simon Booth and Ian Martin scored for the Sea Eagles, but Cronulla ran out winners by 17-12.

Cronulla faced Wests in the major semi-final. Like Manly, Wests had beaten the Sharks in both encounters during the regular season. Greg Pierce and Steve Edmonds scored tries to give Cronulla a 10-4 lead at halftime.

Peter Rowles kicked three penalty goals to level the scores. Midway through the second half, Greg Pierce was sent off following a brawl. He was suspended for the rest of the season.

The Sharks recovered, and Steve Rogers kicked two penalty goals to secure a 14-10 victory. Cronulla were into their second Grand Final.

Manly defeated Wests to earn the right to face Cronulla in the premiership decider. Steve Rogers inherited the captaincy from Greg Pierce, as Cronulla went into the match also without prop forward Dane Sorensen.

The Cronulla side that played in the 1978 Grand Final was Mick Mullane, Rick Bourke, Chris Gardner, Steve Rogers (capt), Steve Edmonds, Dave Chamberlin, Steve Hansard, Barry Andrews, Steve Kneen, Eric Archer, Paul Khan, John McMartin and Gary Stares. Hooker Rowland Beckett came on as a replacement.

Penalty goals from Steve Rogers and Graham Eadie were the only points of the first half. The Sharks went to the break with a 4-2 lead. Steve Edmonds scored the first try of the match, and Cronulla went ahead 7-2.

Just three minutes later, Manly hit back with a try to Tom Mooney. Further penalty goals to Eadie saw Manly sneak ahead 9-7. Eadie and Rogers traded penalty goals late in the game. Rogers levelled the scores at 11-11, which is how the match ended, with no extra time played.

With the Kangaroos squad scheduled to leave for Great Britain, the Grand Final replay was played on the following Tuesday.

The Sharks were hit by injury. Fullback Mick Mullane was replaced by Martin Raftery in a reshuffled backline. John Glossop replaced Barry Andrews at lock, while Peter Ryan and Rowland Beckett came into the side for Gary Stares and John McMartin.

Graham Eadie and Russel Gartner were unstoppable in the first half of the premiership decider. Gartner scored two tries, and Eadie also crossed once, and kicked three goals to give Manly a 15-0 lead at halftime.

A field goal from Eadie was the only point of the second half, and Manly secured their fourth premiership with a 16-0 victory.

The result was heartbreaking for Cronulla. Their effort in the replay without Mullane, McMartin, Stares, Pierce and Sorensen was inspirational; but they came up short against a champion Manly side that was rewarded with seven players in the Australian squad.

Barry Andrews was Cronulla's top point scorer with 133, ahead of Steve Rogers on 129. Mick Mullane was the club's leading try scorer with eleven, one ahead of Steve Rogers and Dave Chamberlin.

1979

Norm Provan entered his second season as Cronulla coach with the bulk of the squad that made the 1978 premiership decider. The Sharks were bolstered by the signing of New Zealand forward Kurt Sorensen.

Cronulla started the season with a 34-7 thumping of Norths. Steve Edmonds scored a hat trick, and Martin Raftery and Steve Rogers both crossed for doubles.

In round two, the Sharks smashed Parramatta 25-0. Steve Edmonds scored two of Cronulla's five tries. They suffered a shock 14-5 loss to Balmain the following week, and went down 16-5 to Easts to be on the verge of dropping out of the top five.

In round five, Cronulla scored four tries to one in a 16-9 win over top of the table Wests, to move back up to third spot.

Kurt Sorensen scored two tries in Cronulla's 16-7 win over Souths. A 16-14 win over Canterbury at Belmore in round seven saw the Sharks with a four way share of the competition lead.

A tough 12-5 win over St George was followed by a six tries to nil 26-6 mauling of Newtown. The win saw Cronulla go to the top of the table.

In round ten, Cronulla faced Manly for the first time since the 1978 Grand Final replay. The Sea Eagles were again too strong, with Graham Eadie the star in a 19-14 win for the Sea Eagles.

Cronulla suffered a shock 17-11 loss to Penrith in round eleven, and turned the midway point of the season in fifth place, but just a win behind competition leaders St George.

Chris Gardner scored a hat trick, and Barry Andrews crossed for a double as Cronulla bounced back with a 26-12 home win over North Sydney.

The Sharks were comprehensively beaten 29-14 by Parramatta in round thirteen. Cronulla fell out of the top five when their round fourteen match against Balmain was postponed due to poor weather.

Cronulla scored five tries, and Steve Edmonds notched seventeen points in a 29-7 win over Easts. They moved back into second spot when Steve Rogers scored sixteen points in a 22-12 win over Wests at Lidcombe.

The Sharks were belted 25-10 by Souths in a major upset; but snuck home 14-12 against Canterbury to stay in third place.

In round nineteen, Cronulla scored four tries to one in an 18-13 win over St George. The Sharks went down 20-6 to Newtown, before smashing Manly by 26-7, with Mick Mullane scoring two of the Sharks' six tries.

The Sharks beat Balmain 14-11 in their postponed match from round fourteen, and finished the regular season in third place after playing an 11-11 draw with Penrith in the final round.

Cronulla faced Parramatta in the first week of the finals. A try from Ron Hilditch gave the Eels a 5-4 halftime lead. Parramatta ran away with the match in the second half, scoring another five tries in a thorough 24-4 victory.

Cronulla were no match for Canterbury in the minor semi-final. The Bulldogs were on a roll that took them all the way to the Grand Final. They scored six tries to three in a 30-15 victory. Mick Mullane, Greg Cox and Rick Bourke were the try scorers for the Sharks.

It was a disappointing end to the season for Cronulla, after going so close to winning the premiership in 1978.

Steve Rogers was Cronulla's top point scorer with 86. Steve Edmonds was the club's leading try scorer with thirteen.

1980

Tommy Bishop returned to Cronulla as coach for the 1980 season, replacing Norm Provan. The appointment was somewhat of a surprise, as Bishop coached North Sydney to the wooden spoon in 1979.

Greg Mullane returned to the Sharks after a stint with Canterbury. Play maker Gavin Miller joined Cronulla from Easts, and Wollongong hooker Barry Pearson signed to replace the retiring John McMartin.

Cronulla opened their campaign with a 16-10 loss to Wests. They bounced back to beat 1979 runners up Canterbury 35-9 on the back of two tries each from Chris Gardner and Rick Bourke.

In round three, the Sharks smashed premiers St George 32-7 at Kogarah. Chris Gardner scored two tries, and Greg Cox notched up seventeen points.

Cronulla suffered an upset 27-10 loss to the previously winless Balmain, before beating Parramatta 14-7 in a touch clash.

Two tries from Gavin Miller, playing at five-eighth, set up an 18-12 win over Souths in round six. Kurt Sorensen scored a double as Cronulla beat Newtown 19-16 the following week.

The Sharks went down 14-11 to Easts, and 15-14 to last placed Penrith; but stayed in the top five with a four tries to one 18-7 win over North Sydney. A hard fought 17-14 loss to Manly in round eleven saw Cronulla in fifth place at the halfway mark of the season.

Cronulla's round twelve match with Souths was postponed due to bad weather. The next week, Cronulla fell out of the top five after going down 16-11 to Wests.

The Sharks went down 13-10 to Canterbury, and 25-12 to St George, before smashing Balmain 33-14 in round sixteen. Gavin Miller scored a double, as did Steve Rogers, who finished the match with 24 points.

Cronulla were soundly beaten 32-7 by Parramatta, before their postponed match with Souths finished in a 6-6 draw. An 11-11 draw with Newtown in round eighteen saw the Sharks in eighth place with four rounds to play; with no chance of making the finals.

In round nineteen, Cronulla suffered their worst defeat in several years when they went down 35-0 to Easts.

Cronulla beat Penrith 19-15, before going down 20-11 to North Sydney. In the final round of the season, the Sharks ended Manly's chances with a seven tries to two 35-12 victory. Greg Mullane scored a double in the win, which saw Cronulla finish the season in ninth spot.

Steve Rogers was Cronulla's top point scorer with 112, ahead of Greg Cox on 52. Greg Mullane was their leading try scorer with nine, one ahead of Chris Gardner.

Greg Pierce retired at the end of the 1980 season. He played 210 first grade matches for the Sharks, and was the first Cronulla player to captain Australia.

Pierce would stay with the Sharks as head coach in 1981, after Tommy Bishop resigned to continue his coaching career in England.

1981

When Greg Pierce took over as coach of Cronulla in 1981, he introduced a policy of promoting rookies, such as Mark Wakefield, David Laming, David Hatch and Ian Forrest.

Centre John Jarvie and halfback Perry Haddock became regular first graders during the season. The Sharks signed former Australian rugby union centre John Berne from Souths to replace the retiring Dave Chamberlin.

Cronulla started life under the coaching of Greg Pierce with a shock 23-12 loss to Penrith. They recovered to beat Norths 24-6, with Mick Mullane scoring two tries.

In round three, Cronulla defeated St George 24-18. Both sides scored four tries, but six goals from Steve Rogers saw the Sharks get home.

Cronulla scored five tries to two in a 23-12 win over Parramatta; and a 12-9 win against Wests saw the Sharks join Easts at the top of the table.

The goal kicking of Steve Rogers again proved the difference as Cronulla beat Balmain 19-13 in round six. The win saw the Sharks go to the outright lead of the competition.

A 21-12 loss to Easts was followed by a 20-15 defeat from Manly saw Cronulla drop to fourth place.

The Sharks went down 12-6 to a resurgent Newtown, but bounced back to defeat premiers Canterbury 19-12 on the back of sixteen points from Steve Rogers.

A 15-15 draw with South Sydney in round eleven saw Cronulla turn the halfway mark of the competition in third place.

Mick Mullane and Rick Bourke each scored two tries as Cronulla beat Penrith 19-10 in round twelve. A 17-16 win over Norths the following week saw the Sharks move up to second spot.

In round fourteen, Cronulla scored six tries to two in a 28-8 win over St George at Kogarah. The Sharks went down 20-5 to Parramatta, but five goals from Steve Rogers helped Cronulla to a 16-15 win over Wests to stay in third place.

Two tries from Mick Mullane helped Cronulla beat Balmain 22-19 at Leichhardt in round seventeen. The next week they snuck home 10-8 over Easts to move within a point of the Roosters at the top of the table.

The Sharks dropped back to third with a 21-12 home loss to Manly; and fell to fourth when they were beaten 14-0 by Newtown.

After a 22-4 loss to Canterbury; Cronulla ended the regular season with an exciting 25-23 win over Souths at Redfern. The Sharks finished in fourth spot.

Cronulla faced Manly in the first week of the finals. Second row forward Bruce Walker scored the only try of the first half to give Manly a 5-2 lead at the break.

The goal kicking of Steve Rogers kept Cronulla in the game, even when Walker scored a second try, and halfback John Gibbs crossed. Rogers scored Cronulla's only try, but it was too late to prevent a 14-11 loss which ended the Sharks' season.

Steve Rogers, who became the second player from Cronulla to captain Australia during the season, topped Cronulla's point scoring list with 194. It was enough for Rogers to also be the competition's leading point scorer in 1981. Rogers was also the Sharks' leading try scorer with fourteen; which was just one behind Easts' Terry Fahey, who was the top scorer in the competition.

1982

Steve Edmonds and Steve Hansard retired at the end of the 1981 season, while Paul Khan returned to Queensland to play for Brisbane Easts. Edmonds and Khan both played more than 110 first grade games for the Sharks, while Hansard played 140 first grade matches in a career with Cronulla and Newtown.

Centre Gary Wright joined the Sharks from Souths, and was joined by Queensland forward Peter McNamara. Cronulla went into the new season in an expanded competition which included teams from Illawarra and Canberra.

The Sharks began their season with a 22-8 win over Balmain, thanks to two tries from Kurt Sorensen. A 13-10 win over Penrith was followed by a 15-8 win over Easts. At the end of round three, Cronulla shared the competition lead with Manly.

Cronulla went down 13-5 to Souths and 10-8 to Wests to drop out of the top five. The Sharks had an 11-11 draw with Norths in round six, before going down 18-7 to Canterbury, 20-11 to St George and 13-7 to Manly to be in ninth spot at the end of round nine.

In round ten, Cronulla smashed newcomers Canberra 44-5. Fullback Mick Mullane scored three of the Sharks' ten tries.

Cronulla beat Newtown 18-9, and Illawarra 19-16, before being thrashed 26-0 by Parramatta in round thirteen. At the halfway mark of the season, the Sharks were in seventh spot; a win short of the top five.

The Sharks went down 9-8 to Newtown, but defeated Balmain 26-11 at Leichhardt. John Jarvie scored two of Cronulla's six tries in round fifteen to be within a point of the top five.

Cronulla snuck home 9-6 against Penrith, but went down 15-7 to Easts in round seventeen. The next week, Cronulla beat Souths 22-12 to remain within a win of the top five.

The Sharks were smashed 32-10 by Wests, and went down 15-12 to Norths to slump to ninth spot at the end of round twenty.

After going down 14-12 to Canterbury, Cronulla beat St George 25-12 on the back of eight goals from Steve Rogers.

The Sharks upset second placed Manly 11-9, before a Mick Mullane hat trick gave Cronulla a 34-5 win over Canberra.

Steve Rogers scored two tries and fourteen points in a 26-8 win over Illawarra in Wollongong, but their late season run was too late to challenge for the finals. Cronulla finished their season with a hard fought 22-17 loss to top of the table Parramatta.

Steve Rogers was again Cronulla's leading point scorer with 187. Kurt Sorensen was the club's top try scorer with eleven, one ahead of Mick Mullane.

1983

Greg Pierce stood down as coach of Cronulla at the end of the 1982 season. He was replaced by former Parramatta coach Terry Fearnley, who had taken the Eels to the Grand Final in 1976 and 1977.

Steve Kneen retired at the end of 1982, while Rick Bourke joined Souths after playing more than 150 first grade games for the Sharks. The biggest loss was the defection of Steve Rogers to St George.

Cronulla signed Wests forwards George Moroko and Paul Merlo, while young backs Dean Carney and Andrew Ettingshausen made their first grade debuts during the season, which saw the increase of the value of a try to four points.

In the opening round of the season, Cronulla were smashed 38-12 by Manly. In round two, the Sharks scored six tries to four in a 36-25 win over Easts.

Cronulla went down 16-12 to Balmain before sneaking home 14-12 against St George. In round five, Chris Gardner scored two tries as the Sharks beat Newtown 26-24 at Campbelltown.

The Sharks went down 24-6 to Canberra at Endeavour, but upset premiers Parramatta 18-14 at Belmore in round seven.

An 18-12 win over Norths saw Cronulla on the cusp of the top five, but a 46-10 belting from Souths saw the Sharks fall back to eighth spot.

Cronulla recovered quickly; scoring seven tries, including doubles to Rowland Beckett and Greg Mullane in a 42-16 win over Wests in round ten.

The next week, Chris Gardner and Steve Hardy each scored twice as the Sharks defeated Penrith 36-12 at Endeavour. A 13-12 loss to Illawarra and a 6-0 win against Canterbury saw Cronulla turn the halfway mark of the season in fourth spot.

Cronulla went down 24-8 to Parramatta, and 32-20 to Manly to drop out of the top five. A 28-7 loss to Easts saw the Sharks drop to seventh place.

The Sharks losing streak continued with a 10-8 loss to Balmain and a 27-18 defeat at the hands of St George. When they lost 17-10 to Newtown in round nineteen, they were in ninth place and their finals chances seemed forlorn.

Cronulla went down 22-14 to Canberra and 14-12 to Norths to stretch their losing streak to eight matches. They finally returned to the winners circle with a four tries to two 23-16 victory over Souths in round 22.

The next week, Cronulla beat Wests 22-18 at Lidcombe. A 20-18 win against Penrith was followed by a 32-24 victory over Illawarra, on the back of two tries from Chris Gardner.

Cronulla finished the season with an 18-6 loss to Canterbury at Belmore, and ended the year in ninth spot, five points short of the top five.

Dane Sorensen was Cronulla's leading point scorer in 1983 with 104. Chris Gardner was the club's top try scorer with seventeen.

At the end of the 1983 season, it was revealed that Cronulla's financial status was in peril. Players had gone unpaid for portions of the season, and at one point it looked as though the Sharks would join Newtown and Wests in not being invited to play in the competition.

1984

Terry Fearnley remained as coach of Cronulla in 1984, as the club battled to resolve their financial issues. Newtown left the competition, but Wests remained after a court injunction.

The New Zealand forwards Kurt and Dane Sorensen left Cronulla to play with Easts in 1984. Greg Mullane left for a second stint at Canterbury, while Mick Mullane announced his retirement. Gavin Miller and John Berne returned to Easts.

The Sharks signed goal kicking winger Tony Armstrong from Canterbury, and veteran forward Des O'Reilly from the Roosters. Rookie backs Jonathan Docking, David Harris and Mark McGaw all made their first grade debuts during the season, as did prop forward Michael Porter.

Cronulla started the season with an 18-14 home loss to Canberra. Ron Giteau scored fourteen points for the Raiders.

The Sharks were trounced 20-0 by Illawarra in round two; but recovered to beat St George 20-12 the next week, thanks to two tries and sixteen points from Tony Armstrong.

Cronulla went down 14-6 to premiers Parramatta, before beating Easts 26-4 in round five. The Sharks scored four tries against a Roosters side that included the Sorensen brothers.

In round six, Cronulla suffered one of their worst ever defeats, going down 50-14 to 1983 runners up Manly at Brookvale Oval. Des Hasler and Col Dreier both scored hat tricks for the Sea Eagles, as the Sharks let in nine tries.

The Sharks bounced back to beat Balmain 32-18. Young hooker David Laming scored two of Cronulla's five tries.

Cronulla went down 24-12 to Penrith and 26-10 to Canterbury, before gaining two valuable points with a round ten bye. The Sharks were smashed 40-16 by Souths, before sneaking home 12-10 against Norths. A 32-6 win over last placed Wests in round thirteen saw the Sharks in tenth place at the midway point of the season.

In round fourteen Cronulla were smashed by a resurgent Canberra side, 38-14. Craig Bellamy scored two of the Raiders' seven tries.

Rookie fullback Jonathan Docking scored two tries in a 16-6 major upset victory over Parramatta; but the Sharks fell 32-22 to St George the next week to halt their momentum.

In round seventeen, Cronulla were trounced 24-8 at home by Illawarra. They followed up with a solid 34-16 win over Easts. Jonathan Docking and Tony Armstrong both scored doubles against the Roosters.

Cronulla went down 20-16 to Manly, and 18-8 to Balmain before playing a 22-22 draw with Penrith in round 21. Lock Greg Nixon scored a double for the Sharks; but their finals chances ended as the slipped to eleventh place.

In round 22, Tony Armstrong scored two of Cronulla's five tries as they upset Canterbury 24-6 at Belmore. Jonathan Docking also crossed for two tries in the win.

After enjoying a week off with the bye, Cronulla went down 20-6 to Souths. They defeated Norths 34-24 in the second last round of the season, and finished their year with a 48-10 mauling of Wests. Chris Gardner scored two of the Sharks' nine tries in a win which saw the club finish the year in tenth spot.

Tony Armstrong was Cronulla's top point scorer with 186. Dean Carney was the club's leading try scorer with twelve.

1985

Terry Fearnley stepped down as coach of Cronulla at the end of the 1984 season, and was replaced by the legendary Jack Gibson. A five time premiership winning coach at Easts and Parramatta, Gibson was seen as the coach who could finally bring the title to the Sharks.

Gibson inherited much the same squad that failed to make the finals under Fearnley, but they were bolstered by the returns of Kurt and Dane Sorensen, and the signings of veteran St George centre Graham Quinn and Wests utility back Wayne Smith.

Goal kicking lock forward Mark Ellison, second row Craig Dimond, and halfback Barry Russell all made their first grade debuts for the club during the season. The Sharks also acquired the services of Great Britain hooker Brian Noble for several matches.

Cronulla started their year with an 18-4 loss to premiers Canterbury. They went down 28-8 to Easts in round two to slump to the bottom of the table.

The Sharks were belted 32-8 by Balmain in round three, and were on their own without a win after losing 16-6 to St George in round four.

In round five, Cronulla broke through for their first win of the season, defeating Illawarra 20-12 at Endeavour. The next week Dean Carney scored two tries and twenty points in a 32-12 home win over Canberra.

Cronulla went down 16-12 to 1984 runners up Parramatta before beating Norths 16-2. The Sharks went down 18-12 to Souths and 8-2 to Penrith before picking up a valuable two points with the bye in round eleven.

In round twelve, Jonathan Docking and Wayne Smith each scored two tries as Cronulla belted Wests 36-18 at Lidcombe.

The Sharks then upset Manly 26-11, with David Hatch scoring two of their four tries. At the halfway mark of the season, Cronulla were in eighth place.

Cronulla went down 24-16 to premiers Canterbury, before beating Balmain 28-8 thanks to two tries from Jonathan Docking.

The Sharks went down 28-10 to top of the table St George; before Barry Russell and winger Phil Hurst each scored two tries in a 28-2 win over Illawarra at Wollongong.

Cronulla snuck home 18-16 against Canberra, and beat Parramatta 26-18 on the back of two tries and fourteen points from Dean Carney.

Cronulla beat Norths 24-12 at the SCG in round 21, but remained three points short of the top five, with five rounds to play.

A 22-20 loss to Souths stalled Cronulla's momentum, and a 24-16 loss to Penrith ended their finals chances.

Cronulla had the bye in round 24, and then smashed Wests 36-10. Jonathan Docking scored two of their six tries, and Dean Carney finished the game with sixteen points.

The Sharks ended their season with a 24-18 loss to Manly, and finished in eighth spot; five points short of the top five.

Dean Carney was Cronulla's top point scorer with 194. He was also the club's leading try scorer with eleven, one ahead of Andrew Ettingshausen.

Kurt Sorensen left Cronulla at the end of the season, and played close to a decade with Widnes in England. He played more than 110 first grade games for the Sharks. Centre or winger Chris Gardner retired after 130 first grade matches for the club.

1986

Jack Gibson remained as head coach of Cronulla in 1986, and brought back Gavin Miller to the club. Miller had spent time in England, and had turned into a clever ball playing back rower.

Former international lock forward Jim Leis joined the club from Canterbury. Gibson elevated wingers Sean Watson and Glenn Coleman, five-eighth Michael Speechley, and centre Mark McGaw to first grade during the season.

Cronulla started their season with a 16-6 win over Easts at the Sports Ground. In round two they were smashed 38-2 by premiers Canterbury at Belmore, conceding six tries.

Andrew Ettingshausen scored two tries in a 14-0 win over Souths; but their season looked set for inconsistency after they went down 26-12 to Canberra in round four.

The Sharks went down 28-6 to Parramatta, 24-12 to Manly and 8-6 to St George to slump to second last, just a win ahead of Canberra.

Cronulla's attack continued to falter, as they were smashed 24-4 by Balmain in round eight. They broke their losing streak with a 28-8 home win against Illawarra.

Cronulla picked up two points from a round ten bye, but they fell 35-18 to Wests, 36-12 to Penrith and 27-6 to Norths to be in last place at the midway point of the season.

The Sharks went down 25-2 to Easts before producing a major upset by beating Canterbury by 18-8. A 14-14 draw with third placed Souths was followed by an 18-4 win against Canberra. Sean Watson scored fourteen points against the Raiders.

In round eighteen, Cronulla produced another upset when they defeated Parramatta 28-14 at the new Parramatta Stadium. Sean Watson scored two of the Sharks' five tries, and finished the match with sixteen points.

Cronulla were belted 32-4 by competition leaders Manly, but bounced back to beat St George 14-6. A 16-14 loss to Balmain was followed by a tough 12-6 away win over Illawarra, and another bye.

The Sharks beat Wests 26-12 on the back of two tries from Andrew Ettingshausen. They were thrashed 50-14 by Penrith, and ended the year in tenth place following a 17-10 loss to Norths.

Sean Watson was Cronulla's leading point scorer with 54, ahead of Phil Hurst on 42. Andrew Ettingshausen was their leading try scorer with nine.

1987

Jack Gibson entered his third season at Cronulla bolstered by the signing of Great Britain forward Mike Gregory and Parramatta five-eighth Ron Quinn. Second rower Alan Wilson became a regular first grader, as did Queensland prop Dan Stains.

Cronulla were well below their best in the opening round, going down 19-2 to Canberra. They bounced back to beat Norths 12-6, and then scored four tries to two in a 22-14 win over St George at the SCG.

The Sharks went down 15-8 to top of the table Balmain in round four, before sneaking home 10-8 against Penrith to move into equal fifth place with Canterbury.

In round six, Glenn Coleman scored a hat trick, and Ron Quinn crossed for two tries in a 34-22 home win over Wests. The next week, a penalty goal from Sean Watson proved the difference when the Sharks beat premiers Parramatta 26-24, which moved Cronulla into fifth place.

A controversial 18-13 win over Manly was followed by a 26-10 loss to Canterbury. In round ten, Sean Watson scored sixteen points in a 28-18 win over Souths.

After having a week off with the bye, Cronulla went down 24-22 to Easts. They defeated Illawarra by 32-12, scoring six tries to one, and turned the midway point of the season in fourth spot.

Cronulla were belted 32-6 by Canberra in round fourteen. They went down 16-6 to Norths and 12-8 to St George to fall out of the top five at the end of round sixteen.

Andrew Ettingshausen scored two of Cronulla's six tries in their 32-26 win over Balmain at Leichhardt Oval, but were still a win outside of the top five.

Mark McGaw scored a hat trick as the Sharks belted Penrith 30-10, and a 28-28 draw with Wests saw Cronulla within a point of the top five.

The Sharks beat Parramatta 16-4 in round twenty to move into equal fifth spot with Souths. They fell back out of the top five after being smashed 30-8 by top of the table Manly.

The Sharks went down 16-4 to Canterbury, and by 16-10 to Souths before picking up two points from the bye in round 24. They were three points short of the top five with just two rounds to play.

Cronulla's finals chances ended with an 18-14 loss to Easts. They went down 24-4 defeat to Illawarra, and finished in eighth spot.

After three years as head coach, Jack Gibson resigned. Although he couldn't manage to get Cronulla into the finals, he will be remembered for fostering the careers of Jonathan Docking and Mark McGaw among others.

Sean Watson was Cronulla's leading point scorer with 106. Glenn Coleman was their top try scorer with ten, one ahead of Jonathan Docking.

1988

After six years of missing the finals, Cronulla fans were hopeful that a new coach could reverse the trend. Former Illawarra coach Alan Fitzgibbon replaced Jack Gibson. A member of the 1969 Balmain premiership winning side, Fitzgibbon had guided the Steelers in their first two years in the competition.

The 1988 competition saw the entry of teams from Brisbane, Newcastle and Gold Coast. The season was reduced to 22 rounds, and byes were eliminated.

Cronulla were quiet on the player transfer market, and Alan Fitzgibbon inherited much the same squad that had failed to fire under Jack Gibson.

The Sharks began their season with a 21-20 home loss to Souths. A field goal from Phil Blake proved the difference for the Rabbitohs.

A 22-18 loss to Canterbury was followed by a 13-12 win over newcomers Gold Coast. A field goal from centre David Burnes secured Cronulla's first win of the season.

An 18-18 draw with Easts was followed by a 38-20 loss to 1987 runners up Canberra. At the end of round five, the Sharks sat in thirteenth place.

Cronulla found their best form in round six, scoring six tries in a 36-18 win over Illawarra. They followed up with a 34-18 victory against St George, with halfback Barry Russell scoring three tries.

Two tries each from Jonathan Docking and Andrew Ettingshausen set up a 38-8 belting of Brisbane, which saw Cronulla rise to seventh spot on the ladder.

In round nine, Cronulla scored five tries to one in a 26-4 away win over Penrith. The following week, Andrew Ettingshausen scored three tries but it wasn't enough to prevent a 44-30 loss to premiers Manly.

Cronulla snuck home 16-14 against Balmain to move into fifth spot at the halfway mark of the season.

A 10-10 draw with Newcastle in round twelve saw Cronulla fall out of the top five. They defeated Parramatta 18-13, before moving back into fifth place with a 42-6 thumping of Wests. Jonathan Docking scored two of the Sharks' eight tries against the last placed Magpies.

A tough 16-12 win over Norths was followed by a 14-12 win over Souths. The narrow victories saw Cronulla move up to fourth place.

The goal kicking of Alan Wilson helped Cronulla get home 18-10 against Canterbury in round seventeen. The win saw the Sharks share the competition lead with the Bulldogs, Canberra and Penrith. They were in third spot on percentages.

Cronulla scored four tries to one in a 26-6 win over Gold Coast, and a 24-6 win over Easts, on the back of two tries from Barry Russell, saw the Sharks at the top of the ladder at the end of round nineteen.

The Sharks scored five tries to two in a comprehensive 32-10 victory over Canberra. Alan Wilson finished the game with sixteen points.

A 22-14 away win over Illawarra, and a hard fought 16-14 win against St George saw Cronulla secure the minor premiership for the first time in their history.

Cronulla enjoyed a week off, and watched Canterbury sneak home 19-18 against Canberra in the first week of the finals.

The experience of the Bulldogs proved too much for Cronulla, who were playing their first finals match since 1981. The Sharks were down 10-4 at halftime, but the Bulldogs were relentless after the break, and ran out winners by 26-8.

Cronulla faced Balmain in the final, with a spot in the premiership decider awaiting the victor. The Tigers had been bolstered by a rare patch of form from Great Britain international Ellery Hanley, and they had disposed of Penrith, Manly and Canberra during the playoffs.

The Sharks were down 3-2 at the break, after a dour first half. True to form, Ellery Hanley proved the difference, scoring the only try of the match in Balmain's 9-2 victory.

Alan Wilson was Cronulla's top point scorer in their best season since 1978 with 167. Andrew Ettingshausen was the club's leading try scorer with seventeen.

1989

Alan Fitzgibbon entered his second season as coach of Cronulla buoyed by their strong performance in 1988. The Sharks had made the finals for the first time since 1981, and only inexperience cost them from making an impression.

Cronulla signed prop forward Danny Lee from Lismore, and veteran Balmain winger John Davidson to bolster their squad.

The Sharks opened their campaign with a 32-14 home win over Canberra. Alan Wilson scored two tries and finished the game with sixteen points.

Cronulla were smashed 22-2 by premiers Canterbury in round two, and went down 12-10 to Souths the next week.

A John Davidson try gave Cronulla a 4-0 win over Easts in round four. They went down 23-22 to St George, before sneaking home 6-4 against Gold Coast in round six.

Alan Wilson scored two of Cronulla's five tries as they defeated Illawarra 26-6 at Wollongong to move into the top five.

A 22-0 thumping of Penrith saw Cronulla move up to fourth spot. Their impressive defence continued with a 26-0 win over Newcastle in round nine.

Cronulla went down 20-10 to Parramatta before beating Norths 20-6 to be in fifth place at the midway point of the season.

The Sharks beat Wests 20-4, before suffering a 42-10 thumping from Brisbane. Despite the loss, they remained in fifth place.

In round fourteen, Cronulla went down 28-6 to Balmain and were joined in equal fifth spot by the Tigers and Parramatta.

Michael Speechley scored two tries in a 19-14 win over struggling Manly, and the Sharks followed up with a 22-16 away win over Canberra.

Glenn Coleman scored two of Cronulla's five tries in their 25-10 win over Canterbury, which saw them move up to third spot. The following week they beat top of the table South Sydney 6-4.

Cronulla suffered a shock 30-12 loss to Easts, but bounced back to beat St George 18-4. An 8-4 loss to Gold Coast bumped the Sharks out of the top five with one round to play.

In the final round of the season, Andrew Ettingshausen scored a club record five tries as the Sharks mauled last placed Illawarra 46-14. The win was enough to secure a playoff for fifth spot against Brisbane.

Cronulla scored six tries to two in a 38-12 thumping of Brisbane to secure fifth spot. Alan Wilson, now playing on the wing, finished the match with eighteen points.

Andrew Ettingshausen scored Cronulla's lone try in their 31-10 loss to Canberra in the first week of the finals. The Sharks were down 16-10 midway through the second half before the Raiders ran away with the match.

Alan Wilson was Cronulla's leading point scorer for the season with 125. Andrew Ettingshausen was their top try scorer with fourteen, three ahead of Wilson.

1990

Dane Sorensen retired at the end of the 1989 season after playing after a club record 216 first grade games. The Sharks signed halfback Laurie Spina from Easts, and Canberra winger Matthew Corkery.

Cronulla began the new decade with a 32-2 thumping of Gold Coast. Winger John Davidson scored two of the Sharks' five tries.

In round two, Cronulla ran in seven tries on their way to a 36-10 thrashing of Souths. The Sharks went to the outright competition lead with a 25-12 win over St George, thanks to six goals from Alan Wilson.

A late penalty goal from Alan Wilson saw Cronulla sneak home 8-7 over premiers Canberra, but they lost for the first time when they went down 18-10 to Canterbury in round five.

The Sharks suffered a shock 26-14 loss to Illawarra, but bounced back to smash Easts 30-2, scoring four tries. Alan Wilson finished the match with eighteen points.

Mark McGaw scored two of Cronulla's five tries in a 30-14 win over Penrith. At the end of round eight, the Sharks were in equal second spot with Canberra, a point behind Canterbury.

The Sharks went down 20-8 to Brisbane and 24-8 to Manly before beating Balmain 18-10. At the halfway mark of the season, Cronulla were in a three way tie for fifth spot.

Cronulla fell out of the top five after going down 10-8 to Newcastle in round twelve. They beat Parramatta 14-8 and Wests 16-10 to move back up to equal fifth place with Manly.

After a 22-6 loss to Norths, Cronulla belted Gold Coast 32-4, with Andrew Ettingshausen scoring two tries. In round seventeen, Jonathan Docking scored a hat trick as Cronulla defeated a struggling Souths side by 36-20.

Cronulla went down 28-6 to St George and 24-10 to Canberra to be three points short of the top five with three games to play.

The Sharks were smashed 38-12 by Canterbury, and 34-0 by Illawarra to end any chances of making the finals. The ended their season with a 16-11 loss to Easts, and finished the year in tenth spot.

Alan Wilson was Cronulla's top point scorer for the season with 102, ahead of Matthew Corkery on 66. Andrew Ettingshausen was the Sharks' leading try scorer with twelve.

Long serving captain and lock forward David Hatch retired at the end of the season after playing close to 190 first grade matches for the club.

John Davidson also retired after playing more than 200 first grade games during a decade long career with Balmain and Cronulla.

1991

Apart from losing John Davidson and David Hatch, Cronulla went into the 1991 season without Laurie Spina, who returned to North Queensland.

The Sharks bought South Sydney and Australian test forward Les Davidson; while rookie centre Paul Bell became a regular first grader during the season.

Cronulla started the season with a 28-8 away loss to Newcastle. The Knights had narrowly missed the finals in 1990, and proved much too strong in the season opener.

In round two, winger Chris Quinn scored two of Cronulla's eight tries in a 44-4 thrashing of Balmain. An 18-14 loss to Easts was followed by an incredible 2-2 draw with Illawarra.

The Sharks then went down 17-10 to 1990 runners up Penrith. In round six, Les Davidson and Andrew Ettingshausen each scored two tries as Cronulla beat Souths 32-18, to be in tenth place.

A 20-20 draw with Canterbury was followed by a 22-6 loss to premiers Canberra. In round nine, Cronulla moved their home match to Perth, and went down 22-12 to Parramatta.

The Sharks were belted 40-2 by Brisbane, with the Broncos running in seven tries. A 19-10 loss to Norths in round eleven left Cronulla in thirteenth place, just one win ahead of last placed Parramatta, at the halfway mark of the season.

In round twelve, Cronulla beat Gold Coast 26-22 in an entertaining match that produced seven tries. The Sharks went down 10-8 to Wests, before Jonathan Docking scored a double in a 22-22 draw with Manly at Brookvale Oval.

Mark McGaw scored two tries, and the goal kicking of young winger Greg Carberry helped Cronulla to a 16-14 win over St George in round fifteen.

The Sharks beat Newcastle 18-10, but a 34-20 loss to Balmain saw an end to any chances of Cronulla making the 1991 finals.

In round eighteen, Cronulla scored ten tries, including a hat trick to Greg Carberry in a 48-14 mauling of Easts. Carberry finished the match with twenty points.

The Sharks were smashed 44-6 by Illawarra at Wollongong. Winger Rod Wishart scored twenty points for the Steelers.

Cronulla upset top of the table Penrith 14-12 in round twenty. A 30-22 win over Souths, inspired by two tries from Mitch Healey, was followed by a last round 26-16 loss to Canterbury. The Sharks finished the year in tenth spot, and were not seriously in the hunt for a top five spot at any point during the season.

Alan Fitzgibbon resigned as coach at the end of 1991 after four years in the role. He will be remembered for guiding the Sharks to their first minor premiership in 1988.

Greg Carberry was Cronulla's leading point scorer for the season with 86, ahead of Alan Wilson on 64. Andrew Ettingshausen and Jonathan Docking were the club's top try scorers with ten apiece.

1992

Legendary Australian captain Arthur Beetson replaced Alan Fitzgibbon as Cronulla coach in 1992. Beetson had coached Easts to within one game of the 1987 Grand Final, and was captain-coach of the Roosters when they went within a win of the 1977 Grand Final.

The Sharks controversially cut Alan Wilson and Jonathan Docking from their roster for the 1992 season. Utility forward David Trewhella joined the club from Easts to play under his former coach, while second row forward Robbie Kearns became a sensation in his first year of first grade.

Cronulla started life under Beetson with a crushing 30-2 loss to Brisbane at Lang Park. A 12-4 loss to Illawarra was followed by a 22-4 defeat at the hands of Newcastle. The Sharks were not only winless after three matches, but had scored just ten points.

Cronulla's attack finally clicked into gear, when they defeated Gold Coast 20-0 in round four. They conceded seven tries in a 40-16 drubbing from 1991 runners up Canberra, before producing a major upset by beating premiers Penrith 18-14 in round six. Halfback Stuart Topper scored a double for the Sharks.

The Sharks were unlucky to go down 23-20 to Manly at Brookvale in round seven. A 20-14 loss to Easts the following week saw Cronulla fall to equal last place with Gold Coast and Parramatta.

Cronulla fell to last place on percentages when they went down 22-10 to Wests in round nine. An 18-6 loss to St George followed.

In round eleven, Cronulla beat Souths 20-16, to move ahead of Gold Coast at the bottom of the table at the midway point of the season.

Cronulla were belted 30-2 by Canterbury in round twelve to again fall to the bottom of the ladder. The next week they beat Norths 18-6 in an uninspiring display.

The Sharks went down 34-10 to Balmain, 26-10 to Parramatta and 20-16 to Brisbane to remain rooted to the bottom of the table.

In round seventeen, Cronulla snuck home 10-6 over Illawarra, before going down 14-6 to high flying Newcastle. The Sharks beat Gold Coast 14-12 thanks to a penalty goal from Mitch Healey, to move safely away from the wooden spoon.

Cronulla upset Canberra 22-4, scoring five tries to one, but went down 18-14 to Penrith in the second last round. The Sharks ended their season with a 28-8 win over Manly, and finished in thirteenth spot.

Mitch Healey was Cronulla's leading point scorer with 58, ahead of rookie centre Lindsay Bowne with 52. Bowne was the club's top try scorer with nine, one ahead of winger Glenn Coleman.

1993

Arthur Beetson remained as Cronulla coach for the 1993 season. Mark McGaw left the club after more than 150 first grade games to join Penrith, while five-eighth Michael Speechley signed with Parramatta.

The Sharks opened their campaign with a hard fought 19-10 home loss to premiers Brisbane. They went down 14-0 to Parramatta and 24-12 to St George. A 28-2 mauling from Canterbury in round four saw the Sharks slump to last place.

In round five, Cronulla conceded nine tries, including doubles to wingers Noa Nadruku and Sean Hoppe, on their way to a 46-6 belting at the hands of Canberra.

The Sharks finally broke through for a win the following week, beating Balmain 18-4. The win saw the Sharks move ahead of the Tigers at the bottom of the ladder.

Cronulla scored five tries to two in a 26-12 away win over Penrith, and continued their revival with a 16-12 win against Souths at the Sydney Football Stadium.

Two tries from centre Paul Bell helped Cronulla to an 18-6 win over Newcastle, but they were then crushed 30-0 by Illawarra.

A four tries to one 20-8 win over Norths saw Cronulla turn the midway point of the season in ninth place; three wins short of the top five.

Cronulla went down 16-8 to Wests and 20-8 by Easts, before beating last placed Gold Coast 24-2 in round fourteen.

The Sharks took another home game to Perth, and went down 26-6 to Manly. They then went down 38-34 to Brisbane, with Mitch Healey scoring two tries and finishing the game with eighteen points. Steve Renouf crossed for a hat trick for the Broncos.

Cronulla beat Parramatta 14-12, and 1992 runners up St George 18-6, before going down 12-0 to top of the table Canterbury.

A 42-12 thrashing at the hands of Canberra was followed by a 14-12 win over struggling Balmain. The Sharks ended the year with a tough 10-6 loss to Penrith, and finished in tenth spot.

Mitch Healey was again Cronulla's top point scorer with 108. Andrew Ettingshausen was the club's leading try scorer with seven.

1994

Arthur Beetson resigned as coach of Cronulla after two years, and was replaced by former test hooker John Lang. Lang won premierships as coach of Brisbane Easts in 1983 and 1991.

Halfback Paul Green followed Lang to Cronulla from Brisbane, while New Zealand centre or winger Richie Barnett also joined the club. Goal kicking winger Eion Crossan also signed with the Sharks.

During the season, fullback David Peachey, prop Adam Ritson and hooker Andrew Neave all became regular first graders.

Cronulla started life under John Lang with a 24-16 win over Canberra, on the back of two tries from Richie Barnett. A Mitch Healey field goal got the Sharks home 15-14 against Canterbury in round two.

Cronulla went down 20-6 to Illawarra, before smashing Wests 36-10 at Campbelltown. Eion Crossan and Andrew Ettingshausen each scored two tries in the win.

In round five, Andrew Ettingshausen scored three tries as Cronulla defeated Manly 26-14. They went down 19-2 to Newcastle, and fell out of the top five with a 16-14 loss to Souths in round seven.

The Sharks were smashed 34-2 by premiers Brisbane, but bounced back to beat Norths 21-14 to stay within a point of the top five.

Six goals from Eion Crossan helped Cronulla to a tough 24-16 win over Balmain, in which both sides scored three tries. A 12-0 loss to Parramatta in round eleven left the Sharks in seventh spot at the halfway point of the season.

In round twelve, Paul Bell scored a hat trick as Cronulla ran in eight tries in a 46-0 thrashing of Gold Coast. Eion Crossan finished the game with eighteen points.

The Sharks went down 26-12 to St George, before beating Easts 20-8 thanks to two tries from Andrew Ettingshausen. Richie Barnett scored two of Cronulla's six tries in a 32-0 win over Penrith, which saw them join Newcastle in fifth place.

A 56-12 belting at the hands of Canberra, was followed by a 14-12 loss to Canterbury; leaving Cronulla in ninth place, but still within a point of the top five, at the end of round seventeen.

Cronulla conceded seven tries in a 42-18 loss to Illawarra at Wollongong; but they stayed in the hunt for a finals berth when Andrew Ettingshausen scored a hat trick in a 32-28 win over Wests.

The Sharks were soundly beaten 38-10 by Manly in round twenty, leaving them three points short of the top five with just two games to play.

Cronulla beat Newcastle 26-4, with Mitch Healey scoring two tries; but it was too little too late for the Sharks. They finished the season in seventh place after beating Souths 42-0 in the last round. Andrew Ettingshausen scored a club record five tries against the Rabbitohs.

Eion Crossan was Cronulla's leading point scorer with 154. Andrew Ettingshausen was easily the club's top try scorer with eighteen.

Cronulla had missed the finals for the fifth year in a row, but had improved significantly under the coaching of John Lang. The Sharks were about to unveil a number of rookies in an attempt to return the club to a premiership threat.

1995

In 1995, the premiership was expanded to include teams from North Queensland, Perth, Auckland, and a second team from South East Queensland. The finals was also extended to the top eight teams.

Intended to be a triumph for ARL chiefs Ken Arthurson and John Quayle, the season was overshadowed by the outbreak of the Super League war, as the introduction of pay television saw a split emerge in the competition.

Cronulla introduced a number of rookies into first grade during the 1995 season. Winger Mat Rogers, prop Craig Greenhill, five-eighth Adam Dykes, lock Nathan Long, centre Paul Donaghy and hooker Dean Treister all made their first grade debuts during the season. New Zealand back rower Tawera Nikau also joined the Sharks. Dan Stains left the Sharks to play with Balmain.

In the opening round, Cronulla went down at home 6-4 to Newcastle in a dour match. They followed up with a 32-18 win over St George at Kogarah. Richie Barnett and second rower Sean Ryan each scored two tries in the win.

In round three, Cronulla suffered a shock 18-14 loss to Perth based Western Reds. In a quirk of scheduling, the sides met again in round four, and Cronulla ran out winners 28-2.

Paul Green scored two tries in a 30-16 win over Balmain, which saw Cronulla move into the top eight at the end of round five.

The Sharks snuck home 11-8 over Penrith, before going down 18-14 to Wests. A 24-0 win over Souths in round eight saw the Sharks in fifth spot.

Paul Donaghy scored two of Cronulla's seven tries in a 40-14 away win over Gold Coast. The Sharks went down 23-18 to Auckland, before beating South Queensland Crushers 20-4 on the back of six goals from Mat Rogers. Cronulla were in fifth place at the halfway mark of the season.

Paul Green scored a double as Cronulla ran in six tries in a 34-10 win over North Queensland Cowboys in round twelve.

A 20-10 loss to St George, and a 26-12 loss to Canterbury saw Cronulla drop to sixth place, as they began to lose touch with the competition leaders.

In round fifteen, Cronulla defeated premiers Canberra 38-12, scoring seven tries to two. They scored another seven in a 36-22 win over Brisbane.

Cronulla scored four tries to two in a 22-10 win over Norths, and then upset top of the table Manly 17-10 at Brookvale Oval.

A 24-14 win over Illawarra was followed by a 48-18 thrashing of Parramatta, with Mitch Healey and Andrew Ettingshausen each scoring two tries, and Mat Rogers scoring twenty points.

Cronulla moved into the top four with a 16-4 win over Easts, who were now known as Sydney Roosters. Mat Rogers scored four tries and twenty points in a 24-14 away win over Newcastle in the final round, and finished in fourth spot.

In their first finals match since 1989, Cronulla faced top of the table Manly. Paul Green, Andrew Ettingshausen and Richie Barnett scored tries to set up a 20-8 lead over the Sea Eagles. Manly hit back with three second half tries to run out winners by 24-20.

Cronulla faced Newcastle in the second week of the finals, and went into the game full of confidence after their solid win over the Knights in the final round of the regular season.

Mat Rogers and Paul Green scored early tries to give the Sharks a 12-0 lead, and they went to halftime ahead 12-6.

A try to Geoff Bell put Cronulla ahead 18-6, but they conceded two late tries to allow the Knights to level the scores. A late field goal from Matthew Johns secured a 19-18 win for Newcastle; ending Cronulla's season.

Despite a disappointing finals campaign, Cronulla had experienced their most successful season since 1988. John Lang had nurtured a number of young players during the season, and the future looked bright for the Sharks.

Mat Rogers was easily Cronulla's leading point scorer for the season with 192. He was also the Sharks' top try scorer with fourteen, two ahead of Andrew Ettingshausen.

<u>1996</u>

John Lang entered his third year as coach of Cronulla with his side in the eye of the storm of the Super League war. Cronulla sided with the breakaway movement, and went into the season without ARL aligned forwards Adam Ritson and Aaron Raper, who both joined Parramatta.

Cronulla signed former North Sydney and Queensland forward Gavin Jones, while Martin Lang joined his father from the Brisbane competition. South African rugby back rower Tiaan Strauss signed with the Sharks, while centre Russell Richardson made his first grade debut during the season.

After the breakaway competition was postponed by a court decision, the Super League aligned clubs refused to play in the first round of the 1996 season. Cronulla forfeited their match against Newcastle.

Common sense prevailed in round two, with all clubs agreeing to compete. Andrew Ettingshausen scored two of Cronulla's five tries in a 24-16 win over St George.

The Sharks went down 19-12 to Western Reds in Perth in round three, but reversed the result with a 26-12 victory in round four.

Mat Rogers and Andrew Ettingshausen each scored two tries, and Rogers racked up twenty points as Cronulla defeated Balmain 36-16.

A 10-2 win over Penrith saw Cronulla rise to fifth spot; but they went down 18-10 to Wests the next week. In round eight, the Sharks beat winless Souths 18-0.

Cronulla beat Gold Coast 18-10, Auckland 28-24, and South Queensland 28-4 to move into equal fourth place at the halfway mark of the season.

The Sharks went down 16-10 to North Queensland, before playing a 20-20 draw with St George. A 16-6 win over Canterbury in round fourteen saw Cronulla move into fourth spot.

Andrew Ettingshausen scored two tries in a 24-16 away win over Canberra, but a 15-12 loss to Brisbane saw the Sharks replaced in the top four by the Broncos.

Cronulla stayed in fifth place with a 15-15 draw with Norths. They squeaked home 12-10 against top of the table Manly, but a 21-14 loss to Illawarra saw their chances of making the top four come to an end.

Mat Rogers and David Peachey each scored two tries in Cronulla's 26-18 win over Parramatta in round twenty. Rogers finished the game with eighteen points. The Sharks beat Sydney Roosters 18-10, and Newcastle 22-0 to finish the season in fifth place.

Cronulla came back from a 12-2 deficit early in the second half to defeat Wests 20-12 in the opening round of the finals. Paul Green scored two tries for the Sharks.

The next week, tries from Andrew Ettingshausen and David Peachey opened up a 12-0 lead for Cronulla in their clash against Brisbane. The Broncos hit back with two tries from Tonie Carroll, but a Richie Barnett try, and superior goal kicking from Mat Rogers saw the Sharks get home 22-16.

Cronulla were bitterly disappointing in their Grand Final qualifier against Manly. The Sea Eagles led just 6-0 at the break, but scored another three tries to run out convincing winners 24-0. They went on to beat St George the following week to claim their sixth premiership.

Mat Rogers was again Cronulla's top point scorer for the season with 150. Veteran centre Andrew Ettingshausen was the club's leading try scorer with thirteen, two ahead of fullback David Peachey.

1997

Rugby league was back in the courts at the end of the 1996 season, and in a surprise decision, the green light was given to the Super League competition to begin in 1997.

Cronulla were part of a ten team competition, alongside Penrith, Canterbury, Canberra, Brisbane, Auckland, North Queensland and the Western Reds, who were simply known as Perth. A team from Newcastle known as the Hunter Mariners were admitted to the breakaway league, as was a side from Adelaide.

The Sharks signed South Queensland utility player Chris McKenna, and St George's prop forward Jason Stevens.

Cronulla started their foray into the brave new world of Super League with a solid 26-4 win over Canberra. Mat Rogers scored a double for the Sharks in the win.

A Mitch Healey field goal gave Cronulla a 13-12 win over Canterbury at Belmore, and they made it three from three with a crushing 34-8 win over Auckland.

Cronulla lost their share of the competition lead when they were belted 38-10 by Penrith in round four. They were edged out 14-12 by Brisbane, but a 20-6 away win over Perth saw them hold onto third spot.

The Sharks went down 16-6 to Canterbury before suffering a shock 29-16 home loss to newcomers Adelaide. A 26-0 win over Hunter, on the back of eighteen points from Mat Rogers, saw Cronulla back in third spot at the halfway mark of the season.

A 22-8 loss to Canberra in round ten saw Cronulla drop to fourth place. They moved back into the top three by scoring seven tries, including doubles to Russell Richardson and Chris McKenna in a 32-2 thrashing of Perth.

Andrew Ettingshausen scored two tries in a 24-10 win over North Queensland, before the Sharks destroyed top of the table Brisbane 32-4, scoring five tries to one.

Cronulla went down 11-8 to Auckland before smashing Penrith 44-20. Mat Rogers scored two tries and 22 points against the Panthers in a win which ensured the Sharks stayed in second spot.

Russell Richardson scored two of Cronulla's six tries in a 28-6 win over Adelaide, and they backed up by scoring another six in a 34-12 win over the Cowboys. In the final round of the season, David Peachey scored a hat trick in Cronulla's 28-16 win over Hunter Mariners. The Sharks finished in second spot.

Mat Rogers was the hero in Cronulla's 22-18 win over Canberra in the major preliminary semi-final. He scored two tries and finished the game with fourteen points.

The Sharks were no match for Brisbane the following week. They conceded five first half tries to be behind 30-2 at the break. The Broncos advanced to the Grand Final with a 34-2 victory.

Mat Rogers scored all of Cronulla's points in their 10-4 win over Canberra in the final. The Sharks earned another crack at Brisbane in the first ever Super League premiership decider.

Cronulla's side for the Grand Final was David Peachey, Mat Rogers, Geoff Bell, Andrew Ettingshausen (capt), Russell Richardson, Mitch Healey, Paul Green, Tawera Nikau, Chris McKenna, Craig Greenhill, Jason Stevens, Dean Treister and Danny Lee. The reserves were Sean Ryan, Adam Dykes, Nathan Long and Les Davidson.

Brisbane centre Steve Renouf scored the only try of the first half, as the Broncos racked up a 10-2 lead at the break.

Russell Richardson scored for the Sharks, but Renouf scored two further tries, and Michael Hancock added another as Brisbane ran out convincing winners by 26-8.

Despite the loss, Cronulla had enjoyed their best season since making the Grand Final in 1978. John Lang achieved a career highlight by coaching the Super League aligned Australian side.

Mat Rogers was Cronulla's top point scorer with 196, just one behind the competition's top scorer, Ryan Girdler of Penrith. Rogers was also the club's leading try scorer with fourteen, three ahead of centre Geoff Bell.

At the end of the 1997 season, the executives of Super League and the Australian Rugby League came to an uneasy reconciliation, ensuring there would be only one competition in 1998. It would include twenty teams under the new banner of National Rugby League.

1998

The first National Rugby League competition consisted of twenty teams, with the top ten making up the finals. Hunter Mariners, Perth and South Queensland Crushers were the casualties from the reconciliation between the Australian Rugby League and Super League; but there would be more to come, as the compromise entailed getting the competition down to fourteen teams by 2000. To make matters harder to achieve that goal, a team from Melbourne was included in 1998.

Cronulla started the season with a 36-14 loss to Sydney Roosters. The Sharks conceded six tries. They bounced back to beat St George 20-14, but went down 26-18 to newcomers Melbourne in round three. Mat Rogers scored a hat trick on his way to notching all eighteen points against the Storm.

Mat Rogers was the sole try scorer in a 6-4 win over Cronulla, but the Sharks remained out of the top ten after going down 24-10 to 1997 ARL premiers Newcastle.

The Sharks went down 11-10 to Balmain, through a field goal from Tigers fullback Shannon Nevin. Russell Richardson scored a double in a 22-12 win over Adelaide.

Cronulla moved into equal tenth spot after beating North Queensland 16-8 in round eight, and followed up with a 20-8 away win over Auckland.

In round ten, Cronulla upset Brisbane 20-10 in their first meeting since the 1997 Super League Grand Final. They were thrashed 32-12 by Manly before beating Norths 16-12 to be in ninth spot at the midway point of the season.

The Sharks went down 18-16 to Newcastle, and by 18-14 to Sydney Roosters, before David Peachey scored two of Cronulla's five tries in a 30-12 win over Souths which kept the Sharks clinging to tenth place.

David Peachey scored another double as Cronulla beat Canterbury 28-6 in round sixteen. The Sharks went down 16-12 to Canberra and 22-12 to Parramatta to fall out of the top ten.

A 14-14 draw with Penrith was followed by a thumping 38-8 victory over Wests at Campbelltown. The Sharks scored six tries to one in a win which saw Cronulla back up to ninth place.

Winger Brett Howland scored two of Cronulla's six tries in a 38-10 thrashing of St George in round 21. The Sharks went down 20-10 to Melbourne, but stayed in the top ten with two rounds to play.

The Sharks were replaced in the top ten by Illawarra after the Steelers upset Cronulla 30-22. The loss was costly, as Cronulla finished the season in eleventh spot, despite a 20-18 away win over Gold Coast in the final round. The Sharks finished one point short of making the finals.

Mat Rogers was again Cronulla's leading point scorer with 148. Brett Howland was the club's top try scorer with thirteen.

1999

After missing out on the 1998 finals, Cronulla were forced into the player transfer market after losing Paul Green to North Queensland, Les Davidson to retirement, and Craig Greenhill to Penrith. The Sharks signed Preston Campbell from the newly defunct Gold Coast, and South Sydney centre Paul Mellor. Andrew Pierce returned to the club after a short stint with Adelaide.

Gold Coast and Adelaide were the victims of the continuing culling of clubs. St George and Illawarra merged to form a new joint franchise club, as the competition was reduced to seventeen teams, and the finals consisted of the top eight.

Cronulla started their season by scoring eight tries in a 44-0 mauling of Balmain. Mat Rogers racked up sixteen points in the win, and Sean Ryan scored two tries.

In round two, Cronulla upset premiers Brisbane by 14-6. The Sharks were top of the table after beating Souths 28-12, thanks to two tries each from wingers Mat Rogers and Brett Howland.

In round four, Cronulla clashed with Brisbane again, and again ran out winners, this time by 20-18. The Sharks remained undefeated after beating Melbourne 20-16, and Canterbury 22-8.

Cronulla suffered their first loss of the season in round seven. They went down 18-16 to Penrith, and were joined at the top of the table by the Panthers, and Sydney Roosters.

Two tries from David Peachey set up a tight 18-16 win over St George-Illawarra. Two points from the bye saw Cronulla return to the outright competition lead, and they stayed on top by beating Souths 27-14 in round ten.

Brett Howland scored a double as Cronulla defeated St George-Illawarra 20-12 at Kogarah; and a Mitch Healey field goal saw the Sharks sneak home 21-20 over Norths.

Cronulla were joined at the top of the table by Sydney Roosters at the midway point of the season. The Sharks lost their round thirteen match to Newcastle by 26-18.

Russell Richardson scored a double as Cronulla beat North Queensland 22-8. The Sharks were soundly beaten 32-14 by Sydney Roosters in round fifteen, conceding six tries.

In round sixteen, Cronulla scored six tries in a 32-4 thrashing of struggling Manly, to return to the outright competition lead.

The Sharks were upset 22-0 by Parramatta; and fell 14-6 to Canterbury before recovering to defeat Canberra 24-8 in round nineteen. Veteran winger Colin Best scored a hat trick against the Raiders.

Cronulla squeaked home 22-20 against Auckland, but a 26-18 loss to Melbourne saw them fall to third place on percentages behind Parramatta and Sydney Roosters.

In round 22, Colin Best and Adam Dykes each scored two tries as Cronulla smashed North Queensland 40-8, running in eight tries.

Cronulla continued their great attacking form by scoring nine tries in a 46-0 win over Wests. Colin Best and Chris McKenna both scored doubles.

The Sharks returned to the competition lead after annihilating North Sydney 56-18. Cronulla scored ten tries, with David Peachey and Andrew Ettingshausen each scoring hat tricks.

Cronulla had the bye in round 25, and wrapped up the minor premiership with a 38-6 win over Penrith. David Peachey scored two of the Sharks' seven tries.

In the first week of the finals, Cronulla faced eighth placed Brisbane. The Sharks proved too strong for the defending premiers. Andrew Ettingshausen, Adam Dykes and Mat Rogers scored first half tries to give the Sharks a 16-2 lead at the break. The Sharks scored another four tries, and Mat Rogers finished the match with 22 points in a 42-20 win.

After enjoying a week off, Cronulla faced St George-Illawarra in the Grand Final qualifier. David Peachey scored the only try of the first half, and Cronulla went to the break with an 8-0 lead. Dragons' five-eighth Anthony Mundine was unstoppable in the second half, scoring three tries to give St George-Illawarra a 24-8 victory. Cronulla were left to lament another missed opportunity.

Mat Rogers was Cronulla's top scorer with 142. David Peachey was the club's leading try scorer with nineteen, one ahead of Brett Howland.

2000

Cronulla were quiet on the player market at the end of the 1999 season. They kept the bulk of the minor premiership winning squad, with the most notable newcomer being young prop forward Chris Beattie from Queensland.

Traditionalists were outraged as Wests and Balmain merged to form the Wests Tigers; and North Sydney and Manly formed an uneasy alliance known as the Northern Eagles. Most offence was taken by the elimination of South Sydney from the new fourteen team competition.

Cronulla started their campaign with a 28-12 win over 1999 runners up St George-Illawarra. Colin Best scored two of the Sharks' five tries.

David Peachey scored two tries in Cronulla's 28-2 thumping of Sydney Roosters in round two. The next week Cronulla were beaten 19-18 by Parramatta thanks to a field goal from Eels halfback David Penna.

Cronulla went down 18-14 to Brisbane, but bounced back to beat North Queensland 26-12 to move up to fourth place.

The Sharks had a tough 14-4 win over Canterbury, before being smashed 30-2 to Northern Eagles. A 26-14 win over Melbourne in round eight saw Cronulla in third spot.

Cronulla went down 16-12 to Wests Tigers, and to Canberra by 24-18 to fall to fifth spot. In round eleven, Mat Rogers scored three tries and 26 points in a 42-16 thumping of Newcastle.

The Sharks went down 24-20 to Auckland, and by 16-14 to Sydney Roosters to turn the halfway mark of the competition in seventh place.

In round fourteen, Cronulla scored six tries to one in a 28-8 win over Northern Eagles. The next week they went down 28-26 to Penrith, and dropped out of the top eight.

In a tight competition, Cronulla went back up to sixth place by beating Canberra 26-18. A 32-4 loss to top of the table Brisbane saw the Sharks again drop out of the top eight.

In round eighteen, rookie halfback Blaine Stanley scored two tries and seven goals in a 42-6 thrashing of North Queensland. The win saw the Sharks in ninth place, one point outside of the top eight.

David Peachey scored a hat trick as Cronulla defeated Canterbury 26-14. The Sharks moved up to seventh place, and went up to fifth after thrashing St George-Illawarra 40-10. Andrew Ettingshausen and Chris McKenna each scored two tries against the Dragons.

Cronulla went down 22-16 to premiers Melbourne, and 24-22 to Wests Tigers, to again fall out of the top eight with four rounds to play.

Two tries from Colin Best helped the Sharks to a tough 22-12 win over Auckland. After going down 20-16 to Newcastle, Cronulla beat Parramatta by 34-18, with Mat Rogers scoring a hat trick in his 22 points. The win saw the Sharks in eighth spot.

In the final round of the regular season, Cronulla were smashed 44-6 by Penrith, conceding eight tries. Despite the loss, the Sharks limped into the finals in eighth place.

Cronulla fought hard in their finals encounter against Brisbane, but ultimately had their season ended by a 34-20 loss. Brisbane went on to win the premiership.

Yet again, Mat Rogers was Cronulla's leading point scorer with 212. He was also the club's top try scorer with eighteen.

2001

At the end of the 2000 season, club legends Andrew Ettingshausen and Mitch Healey retired. Ettingshausen played a club record 328 first grade matches, and scored 165 tries. Healey played more than 220 first grade games for the Sharks.

Cronulla were again quiet on the transfer market; with young forwards Nick Graham and Luke Stuart stepping up to be among the most consistent players in the competition. Halfback Jason Ferris became a lynch pin of the side, and rookie forward Paul Gallen made his first grade debut during the season.

Cronulla were smashed 30-6 by St George-Illawarra in the opening round. They recovered to beat Parramatta 13-12 in round two, thanks to an Adam Dykes field goal.

Colin Best scored two tries as Cronulla beat Canberra 18-12, but they went down 34-24, despite Preston Campbell scoring two tries from fullback.

In round five, Cronulla defeated North Queensland 24-16 to move into the top eight. The next week, Russell Richardson and Adam Dykes each scored two tries as the Sharks beat Penrith 31-12 to move up to fourth spot.

The goal kicking of Jason Ferris proved the difference as Cronulla beat Northern Eagles in Gosford in round seven. The win saw Cronulla join Brisbane at the top of the table.

Cronulla fell back to fourth place with a 22-13 loss to Sydney Roosters, and were in danger of falling out of the top eight after going down 22-12 to Newcastle.

Cronulla scored five tries to three in a 26-16 win over the newly christened New Zealand Warriors. They were belted 35-16 by Brisbane in round eleven; and then went down 20-6 to Canterbury. A 16-16 draw with Wests Tigers saw the Sharks in sixth place at the halfway mark of the season.

In round fourteen, Cronulla played another draw, as their exciting match with St George-Illawarra ended at 26-26, with both sides scoring four tries.

Cronulla fell out of the top eight after being thrashed 36-6 by Parramatta, conceding seven tries. They bounced back to score five tries to one in a 26-12 away win over Canberra.

Young winger Damien Mostyn scored three of Cronulla's seven tries in a 40-18 surprise win over Melbourne. The win saw the Sharks back up to sixth place.

In round eighteen, halfback Preston Campbell scored a hat trick, and Paul Mellor crossed twice, as Cronulla belted North Queensland 36-6 in Townsville.

The Sharks revival continued, when they ran in eight tries, including a double to Preston Campbell, as they thrashed Penrith 42-10 to move up to fifth.

Chris McKenna scored a hat trick as Cronulla scored nine tries in a 40-18 win over Northern Eagles. They had a solid 22-14 win over Sydney Roosters in round 21, before scoring eight tries in a 49-30 win over Newcastle. David Peachey scored a hat trick against the Knights in a win which moved Cronulla into the top four.

The Sharks suffered a shock 30-0 loss to the Warriors, but bounced back to beat Brisbane 24-16. They went down 16-14 to Canterbury, and finished in fourth place after beating Wests Tigers 36-12.

Paul Mellor scored three tries as Cronulla defeated Brisbane 22-6 in the first week of the finals. The following week, the Sharks romped to a 52-10 win over Canterbury, with Preston Campbell and Jason Ferris each scoring two tries.

Cronulla led Newcastle 10-6 at halftime in their Grand Final qualifier. The Knights rallied to end the Sharks' season with an 18-10 victory. They won the premiership the next week.

Yet again, Cronulla ended the season with the disappointment of not progressing to the premiership decider. After eight years in the role, John Lang resigned as coach, and resumed his career with Penrith.

Jason Ferris was Cronulla's top point scorer in 2001 with 121, just ahead of Preston Campbell with 116. Campbell was also the club's leading try scorer with seventeen; four ahead of Adam Dykes.

At the end of the 2001 season, Mat Rogers announced his switch to rugby union. He played more than 120 first grade matches for Cronulla, and scored over 1100 points; second in the history of the club behind his father Steve.

2002

Chris Anderson was appointed coach of Cronulla for the 2002 season. Anderson had won a premiership as a player with Canterbury, and represented Australia. He coached Canterbury to an unlikely premiership victory in 1995, and was at the helm of Melbourne when they won the competition in 1999, in just their second season.

Halfback Brett Kimmorley joined Cronulla from Northern Eagles. He had won a premiership under Anderson at Melbourne. Kimmorley was joined by Northern Eagles back rower Phil Bailey, and Penrith winger Matthew Rieck.

Newcastle five-eighth Matthew Johns returned to Australia after a season with Wigan, and lent great experience to the Sharks. Maitland junior lock forward Greg Bird made his first grade debut for the club, while former South Queensland Crushers prop forward Danny Nutley completed the Sharks' recruitment.

The 2002 competition was expanded to fifteen teams, as South Sydney returned after winning their right to compete in the courts.

Cronulla began their season with a 24-18 win over St George-Illawarra, on the back of two tries from David Peachey.

The Sharks ran in six tries in a 30-24 win over Melbourne in round two. Cronulla joined premiers Newcastle at the top of the table after beating Penrith 18-10 in round three.

Cronulla went down 18-16 to Brisbane in round four, before beating Wests Tigers 36-30, with Preston Campbell, now playing winger, scoring two tries.

In round six, Cronulla faced premiers Newcastle, and were humiliated 52-8, conceding nine tries. Andrew Johns finished the game with twenty points.

The Sharks suffered a heavy 30-10 defeat from Canterbury, and were belted 36-10 by Canberra to fall out of the top eight at the end of round eight.

When Cronulla went down 36-6 to Parramatta, they had conceded more than 150 points in their last four games. Their poor defensive display continued with a 48-22 loss to Canterbury. Centre Nigel Vagana scored a hat trick for the Bulldogs.

The Sharks slumped to twelfth place after going down 24-22 to Penrith. They went down 42-20 to the Warriors, but broke their losing streak by beating St George-Illawarra 34-13 in round thirteen. They remained twelfth at the midway point of the season.

Two tries and twenty points from Brett Kimmorley helped Cronulla to a 36-26 win over Canberra which moved the Sharks back into eighth spot. In round fifteen, Paul Mellor scored two of Cronulla's eight tries as they thrashed the Cowboys 46-16.

After a week off with the bye, the Sharks beat the Warriors 36-24 on the back of two tries from David Peachey. A Brett Kimmorley field goal was the difference as Cronulla beat Parramatta 25-24 in round eighteen.

David Peachey and Matthew Rieck each scored doubles as the Sharks smashed Northern Eagles by 46-24. Paul Mellor scored a double the next week as Cronulla beat Souths 22-6.

Cronulla moved up to fifth place with a 34-20 win over Sydney Roosters. They smashed Newcastle the next week, scoring eleven tries in a 64-14 victory. Matthew Rieck scored a hat trick, while Brett Kimmorley, David Peachey and Paul Mellor each scored doubles. Kimmorley finished the game with a club record 28 points.

Chris McKenna scored two of Cronulla's six tries in a 34-18 win over Wests Tigers. The Sharks moved into fourth place when Canterbury were stripped of their points due to salary cap breaches.

David Peachey scored a hat trick as Cronulla defeated North Queensland 36-14 in round 23. Young five-eighth Jye Mullane scored a double.

Cronulla picked up another two points from the bye, but dropped to fifth spot after going down by 30-18 to Sydney Roosters in the final round.

The Roosters and Cronulla met again in the first week of the finals. Two tries from Matthew Rieck helped Cronulla to an 8-0 lead at halftime. The Roosters raced to a 26-8 lead midway through the second half, and hung on to win 32-20. Rieck finished the match with three tries.

Cronulla faced St George-Illawarra the following week. Matthew Johns suffered a back injury in the first ten minutes which ultimately ended his career. Tries to David Peachey, Phil Bailey and Paul Franze set up an 18-12 halftime lead for the Sharks. Both sides forgot about defence in the second half, and Cronulla hung on to win 40-24.

Yet again, Cronulla fell in the Grand Final qualifier. They went down 16-10 to the Warriors; but the season could be viewed as a success after a poor start.

Brett Kimmorley scored a club record 251 points in 2002. David Peachey was Cronulla's leading try scorer with seventeen, three ahead of Kimmorley.

2003

At the end of 2002, veteran centre Colin Best, and Queensland back rower Chris McKenna left the Sharks to continue their careers in England. Matthew Johns announced his retirement after a career which included a premiership win with Newcastle in 1997. Preston Campbell signed with Penrith.

In their opening match, against Melbourne, thirteen tries were scored as the Storm ran out winners 36-30 in a match that entertained fans of attacking play. The Sharks had a bye in round two, and were belted 30-4 by Brisbane, and 40-20 by premiers Sydney Roosters to fall to second last spot at the end of round four.

Cronulla suffered a second loss to Melbourne, going down 18-12; before losing 32-24 to Newcastle. They had a second bye in round seven, but went down 28-12 to St George-Illawarra the next week.

Cronulla broke through for their first win of the season in round nine, beating Manly 40-16. The Sea Eagles were back in the competition as a sole entity after the Northern Eagles franchise dissolved at the end of 2002. Rookie hooker Matt Hilder scored two of the Sharks' eight tries.

The Sharks then best last placed South Sydney by 30-14, before a hat trick from Brett Kimmorley set up a 30-24 away win over Newcastle.

Cronulla went down 20-14 to Canberra, and 23-6 to the Warriors to be in twelfth spot at the halfway mark of the competition.

Phil Bailey scored a double in a 28-26 win over Wests Tigers, before the Sharks went down 36-18 to Manly at Brookvale Oval in round fifteen.

The next week, Phil Bailey again crossed for two tries, as the Sharks beat North Queensland 34-28. However, they remained inconsistent, going down 20-0 to Penrith and 44-12 to Wests Tigers.

The Sharks went down 31-24 to the Warriors in round nineteen, and slumped back to second last spot. A 40-12 thrashing at the hands of Canberra was followed by an upset 20-10 win over Brisbane. Phil Bailey was again the star, scoring two tries.

Cronulla went down 36-28 to top of the table Sydney Roosters in round 22, before having a five tries to three 25-16 win over St George-Illawarra.

In round 24, Cronulla experienced their worst ever loss. The Sharks were utterly humiliated, conceding fourteen tries in a 74-4 loss to Parramatta. Jamie Lyon scored five tries.

Incredibly, Cronulla immediately bounced back to hand out a thrashing of their own. Though their defence was still suspect, the Sharks ran in ten tries, including a hat trick to interchange player Sam Isemonger, on their way to a 54-34 win over Souths. Winger Jarrad Anderson scored eighteen points in the win.

Cronulla finished a disappointing season with a hard fought 28-14 loss to Canterbury. The Sharks ended the year in twelfth spot.

Jarrad Anderson was Cronulla's leading point scorer for the season with 94, ahead of Brett Kimmorley on 74. Phil Bailey was the club's top try scorer with thirteen.

Cronulla had suffered a horrific injury toll during the 2003 season, which resulted in them using 36 players in first grade. It did provide an opportunity for winger David Simmons and prop forward Keith Galloway to make their first grade debuts.

Chris Anderson resigned as coach of Cronulla at the end of the 2003 season. Anderson had great success as coach of Australia, and finished his club career with the Sydney Roosters in 2007.

2004

Stuart Raper replaced Chris Anderson as head coach at Cronulla for the 2004 season. The squad was strengthened by the signings of prop Andrew Lomu form Easts, and prolific try scorers Nathan Merritt from Souths, and Nigel Vagana from Canterbury.

In the first round of the new season, Cronulla went down 12-6 to Wests Tigers in a dour match. The Sharks were beaten 24-20 by Canterbury, before finding their first win with a 28-20 victory against Manly, with David Peachey and Brett Kimmorley each scoring two tries.

In round four, Cronulla were thrashed 36-12 by a resurgent South Sydney. A 36-10 home loss to North Queensland saw the Sharks at the bottom of the table.

David Peachey scored two of Cronulla's six tries as they upset Canberra 38-24. Brett Kimmorley kicked seven goals in the win.

The Sharks beat Parramatta 18-14 in golden point extra time, but were thrashed 42-12 by St George-Illawarra. They bounced back to score seven tries in a 36-26 away win over Melbourne.

Cronulla were crushed 38-18 by Sydney Roosters, but defeated Manly 30-28 at Brookvale in round eleven. Paul Gallen, playing at five-eighth, scored two tries.

Rookie centre Ryan McGoldrick, and hooker Michael Sullivan both scored two tries as Cronulla beat Souths 38-18, and a shock 30-22 away win against Brisbane saw the Sharks in the top eight for the first time of the year. They clung to eighth spot at the midway point of the season.

Cronulla went down 26-16 to Canberra, and 32-12 to premiers Penrith before picking up two points from a bye in round sixteen.

The Sharks moved back into the top eight with a 34-26 away win over Newcastle. Winger Matthew Rieck scored two of the Sharks' six tries.

Cronulla beat the Warriors 22-14, and retained eight spot despite a 37-26 loss to Canterbury. Bulldogs winger Hazem El Masri scored a hat trick.

The Sharks fell to ninth place after going down to St George-Illawarra 24-16 in round twenty. A 16-12 home loss to Brisbane saw them drop to eleventh.

A 26-12 upset win over top of the table Sydney Roosters was followed by a 44-22 loss to struggling Parramatta, emphasising Cronulla's inconsistencies.

After another bye, Cronulla went down 36-28 to Melbourne, and 36-20 to North Queensland to finish their season in eleventh place; just one win short of the finals.

Brett Kimmorley was Cronulla's leading point scorer with 92, ahead of goal kicking hooker Matt Hilder on 84. Nigel Vagana was the Sharks' top try scorer in his first season with the club. He scored twelve, two ahead of Matthew Rieck. Young winger David Simmons scored nine, as did veteran fullback David Peachey.

2005

After missing the finals for three consecutive seasons, Cronulla were quiet in the player transfer market at the end of 2004. They lost prop Chris Beattie to England, and their main signings were goal kicking winger Luke Covell from Wests Tigers, and five-eighth Adam Dykes, who returned to the club after mixed success at Parramatta. Forwards Kevin Kingston and Beau Scott made their debuts during the season.

Cronulla started their season with a tough 20-14 win over Penrith. In round two, they were belted 46-20 by Manly, conceding eight tries.

The Sharks beat Parramatta 18-10, and premiers Canterbury 26-12, before smashing North Queensland 38-6. David Simmons scored two of their seven tries against the Cowboys.

Cronulla gained a share of the competition lead in round six by picking up two points from the bye. They quickly dropped to third with a 16-12 loss to Brisbane.

At the end of round eight, five teams were equal at the top of the ladder, including Cronulla. They defeated Melbourne 30-10, and stayed on top with a 28-24 win over the Warriors in Perth.

In round ten, six goals from Luke Covell proved the difference as Cronulla beat Canberra 32-26. Two tries each from Covell and Paul Mellor set up a solid 30-22 win over Penrith.

The Sharks lost their share of the lead after going down 34-26 to Parramatta in round twelve. Cronulla experienced a 56-14 thumping from North Queensland the next week to turn the midway point of the season in fifth spot.

Cronulla were beaten 34-18 by Wests Tigers before they edged out Sydney Roosters 16-10 in a touch encounter. A round sixteen bye saw the Sharks back in the top four.

The Sharks went down 22-10 away to Brisbane, and 22-14 to Souths, before beating Newcastle 30-26 in golden point extra time. Nathan Merritt scored two tries and fourteen points against the Knights.

Cronulla dropped to seventh on percentages after going down 20-10 to St George-Illawarra in round twenty, but were in a six way tie for third place.

The Sharks were belted 46-6 by Wests Tigers, with Scott Prince scoring a hat trick. Incredibly, the next week Cronulla beat Melbourne 40-16, with David Simmons scoring two of their seven tries.

A 14-8 loss to Sydney Roosters was followed by a 68-6 annihilation of Manly. Nigel Vagana and Brett Kimmorley each scored hat tricks as the Sharks ran in twelve tries in the biggest win in the club's history.

Cronulla went down 44-14 to Newcastle, and 26-22 to Souths to end their season in seventh place. They drew St George-Illawarra in the first week of the finals, and came up just short. Former Cronulla centre Colin Best scored two tries for the Dragons on their way to a 28-22 victory, which ended Cronulla's season.

Luke Covell was the Sharks' leading point scorer with 186. David Simmons was their top try scorer with sixteen, four ahead of Nigel Vagana.

2006

Stuart Raper started his third year as coach of Cronulla without veteran fullback David Peachey, who left the club to play with Widens in England after more than 230 first grade games for the Sharks.

Keith Galloway also left Cronulla to play for Wests Tigers. Winger Nathan Merritt returned to South Sydney. The Sharks signed former Newcastle winger Darren Albert, St George second rower Lance Thompson, Souths halfback Brett Kearney, and Penrith prop Ben Ross. Prop forward Luke Douglas became a regular first grader during the season.

Cronulla had the bye in the first round of the season, and opened their campaign with a 16-12 loss to Brisbane. They went down 20-18 to Manly, before beating Souths 24-22 in round four to record their first win of the season.

The Sharks went down 28-24 to Sydney Roosters before being thumped 42-16 by premiers Wests Tigers. In round seven, they snuck home 24-22 against 2005 runners up North Queensland.

Luke Covell scored two tries and twenty points, and Darren Albert also crossed for a double as Cronulla beat Penrith 40-12 to move into the top eight.

The Sharks scored five tries to two in a 30-12 win against St George-Illawarra, and then moved up to sixth spot with a 38-28 away win over Canberra.

Cronulla went down 32-24 to Canterbury, but recovered to defeat the Warriors 34-20, with Darren Albert again scoring two tries. A round thirteen bye saw the Sharks in seventh spot at the halfway mark of the competition.

A 26-4 away win over the Cowboys saw the Sharks move into the top four. They best Manly 15-12 and Newcastle 26-16 to be equal second with Brisbane at the end of round sixteen.

Cronulla went down 26-12 to the Broncos, and fell out of the top four after going down 22-10 to Wests Tigers. A 38-32 loss to Sydney Roosters was followed by a 28-12 defeat at the hands of Melbourne, and the Sharks' spot in the top eight suddenly became vulnerable.

In round 21, Cronulla lost their fifth match in a row, going down 22-18 to Newcastle. The next week they went down 12-10 to the Warriors and slipped out of the top eight.

Cronulla were smashed 34-14 by Parramatta, and made it eight losses in a row when they went down 32-28 to Penrith, ending their finals chances.

In round 25, Cronulla went down 18-4 to St George-Illawarra. They finished the season with a 26-24 home loss to Canberra, and ended the year in thirteenth place.

Ten consecutive losses to end the season spelt the end of Stuart Raper's term as head coach. He was replaced by Ricky Stuart for the 2007 season.

2006 will be remembered for the inexplicable loss of form in the second half of the season. Cronulla looked set to challenge for the minor premiership before the loss of form saw them finish third last.

Luke Covell was again Cronulla's leading point scorer with 192. Darren Albert was their top try scorer with twelve.

The appointment of Ricky Stuart gave hope to the Cronulla faithful. Stuart had won three premierships as a player with Canberra, and had taken the Sydney Roosters to the premiership in his first year as coach in 2002.

2007

At the end of 2006, Nigel Vagana signed with South Sydney, and Phil Bailey went to Wigan; robbing Cronulla of two of their strike attacking players.

Ben Pomeroy became a key player in the centres, while Isaac De Gois shared the hooking duties with Kevin Kingston to give the Sharks a variety of attacking options.

Cronulla started life under Ricky Stuart with an 18-0 win over Penrith, anchored by two tries from new fullback Brett Kearney.

In round two, the Sharks went down 18-16 to the newest incarnation of a side from the Gold Coast. Former Sharks star Preston Campbell scored a try and kicked three goals for the newly christened Titans.

Cronulla went down 26-16 to Souths, before unleashing their best attack in a 40-4 thumping of St George-Illawarra. Brett Kearney scored a hat trick, and Ben Pomeroy crossed twice against the Dragons.

The Sharks followed up with a tough 14-12 loss to Wests Tigers, but in round six, they trounced Canberra 26-0, with Ben Pomeroy scoring three tries.

Cronulla went down 20-16 to Newcastle, before beating the Warriors in Auckland 22-20 to move up to fifth spot. A 16-8 win over Brisbane in round nine saw the Sharks move into the top four.

A 30-20 win over Canterbury saw Cronulla in third place, but they dropped to fifth after going down 13-12 to Sydney Roosters in golden point, thanks to a field goal from Anthony Minichiello.

Cronulla went down 26-24 to North Queensland, but beat St George-Illawarra 20-16 to be in fifth spot at the halfway mark of the season.

The Sharks went down 12-2 to the Warriors, and 16-12 to Souths, before two points from a round sixteen bye kept their spot in the top eight. A hard fought 14-12 loss to Canterbury saw the Sharks drop down to tenth spot.

In round eighteen, Cronulla went down 23-12 to a struggling Sydney Roosters side. A 29-22 loss to Manly and a 30-16 defeat from Brisbane saw the Sharks drop to fourteenth; three wins outside of the top eight with five rounds to play.

A field goal from Cooper Cronk gave Melbourne a 17-16 win over the Sharks in round 21. The next week it was a Brett Seymour field goal in golden point extra time that gave Cronulla a 25-24 win over Parramatta.

For the third week in a row, Cronulla's match was decided by a field goal. Wests Tigers' hooker Robbie Farah kicked the decisive one pointer in a 29-28 victory.

In round 24, Cronulla scored five tries to two in a 28-12 win over Gold Coast. They beat Canberra by 22-12 the next week to be a win short of the top eight, finishing the season in eleventh spot.

Luke Covell was again Cronulla's leading point scorer with 176. Ben Pomeroy was the club's top try scorer with twelve, two ahead of Covell. Greg Bird and David Simmons both scored nine tries.

2008

Cronulla were quiet on the player transfer market at the end of 2007. Ricky Stuart introduced prop Kade Snowden and utility playmaker Blake Green into first grade, but was otherwise confident in the 2007 squad.

The Sharks started their season with an impressive 16-10 win over 2007 runners up Manly at Brookvale Oval. The goal kicking of Luke Covell proved the difference.

In round two, Brett Kimmorley kicked a field goal against his former club Melbourne to give Cronulla a 17-16 win. They went down 18-4 to Gold Coast before beating St George-Illawarra 18-16 in golden point in round four.

Cronulla snuck home 12-10 against Souths before going down 21-20 to Penrith in another golden point match. The Sharks went down 20-16 to Wests Tigers in round seven, and were on the verge of falling out of the top eight.

A bye, and a 24-18 away win over North Queensland helped keep the Sharks in sixth spot. They moved up to fifth with a 13-6 win over Brisbane, but dropped back to eighth after going down 30-22 to Canterbury in round eleven.

Luke Covell and Ben Pomeroy each scored two tries as Cronulla defeated Gold Coast 30-14, and they sat in fifth spot at the midway point of the season after beating Penrith 24-22, thanks to a hat trick from Luke Covell.

Two tries from David Simmons helped Cronulla to a 24-8 win over the Warriors. Cronulla moved back into the top four after a tough 16-14 win over Parramatta, and Luke Covell scored twenty points in a 36-24 win over Canberra, which saw the Sharks in third spot at the end of round sixteen.

Cronulla picked up a further two points from the bye before being smashed 34-6 by top of the table Manly. A hard fought 16-13 win over Newcastle was followed by an 18-12 loss to Brisbane. The Sharks were in fourth spot at the end of round twenty.

A field goal from Brett Kimmorley got the Sharks home 13-12 against St George-Illawarra. The next week Ben Pomeroy scored two of Cronulla's five tries in their 28-14 win over Souths.

A shock 18-4 away loss to the Warriors was forgotten after Cronulla belted Sydney Roosters by 20-0 in round 24. After beating Wests Tigers 32-6 at Leichhardt, the Sharks finished the regular season with a 28-22 win over North Queensland. They finished third on percentages, behind Melbourne and Manly.

Winger Misi Taulapapa scored a hat trick as Cronulla ran in seven tries in a 36-10 blitzing of Canberra in the first week of the finals. They enjoyed a week off before their season came to an end with a 28-0 loss at the hands of Melbourne.

Luke Covell was the competition's leading point scorer with 206. He was also Cronulla's top try scorer for the year with fifteen.

2009

Ricky Stuart's team had gone close in 2008, with just a touch of class from Melbourne keeping them from the premiership decider. The Sharks entered the new season without key playmakers Greg Bird, who moved to France; and Brett Kimmorley, who joined Canterbury. They also lost hookers Kevin Kingston to Parramatta, and Isaac De Gois to Newcastle. Veteran second row forward Lance Thompson retired at the end of 2008.

The Sharks signed former test five-eighth Trent Barrett, Sydney Roosters back rower Anthony Tupou, and long serving Canterbury hooker Corey Hughes. They also had some exciting rookie backs such as Matthew Wright and Blake Ferguson.

Cronulla started well enough, beating Penrith by 18-10, before going down 24-12 to Newcastle the next week. Their attack was called into question after a 10-6 loss to St George-Illawarra in round three, as they started to feel the loss of so many playmakers.

A 24-12 loss to Canterbury was followed by a 24-14 defeat at the hands of Canberra. At the end of round five, Cronulla sat last on the competition table.

In round six, Cronulla conceded six tries in a 34-10 loss to North Queensland, in Adelaide. They went down 32-26 to Souths and 19-12 to Sydney Roosters before reassessing during their bye week in round nine.

Two tries from Anthony Tupou wasn't enough in a 26-22 loss to Penrith, and the Sharks were soundly beaten 26-4 by St George-Illawarra in round eleven.

Cronulla upset Parramatta 13-10, and an 18-10 win over the Warriors saw them rise to equal last with Sydney Roosters at the midway point of the season.

Paul Gallen scored two tries as Cronulla edged out Canberra 24-22, to win their third game in a row. There were thoughts of a miracle recovery when the Sharks belted Brisbane 46-12 in round fifteen, with Blake Ferguson crossing for three tries.

The revival ended with a 19-12 loss to the Roosters, and a 24-4 defeat from North Queensland. Only the bye in round eighteen saved the Sharks from again falling to last place.

In round nineteen, Cronulla pushed premiers Manly all the way, but went down 32-26. Ben Pomeroy scored a double against the Sea Eagles.

A 30-10 drubbing from Melbourne was followed by a 30-0 mauling from Parramatta. The Sharks were back in equal last spot with the Roosters with five rounds to play.

Cronulla went down 30-10 to Brisbane, and by a whopping 56-10 to Wests Tigers, and it seemed as though the end of the season could not come quickly enough.

The Sharks lost 20-10 to Gold Coast, 18-16 to Manly and 26-24 to Souths to end a miserable season. They avoided the wooden spoon only as Sydney Roosters had a worst for and against record.

The loss of experienced playmakers Kimmorley and Bird was too much to overcome, despite patches of good form from Trent Barrett. However, the dramatic form reversal from 2008 saw Ricky Stuart start to come under pressure.

Luke Covell was once again Cronulla's top point scorer with 134. Rookie Blake Ferguson was the club's leading try scorer with nine, one ahead of Covell. Paul Gallen finished the year with seven tries.

2010

David Simmons left Cronulla at the end of 2009 to join Penrith. A reliable winger with a prolific try scoring rate, Simmons had lost his place in the Sharks side due to the rise of Blake Ferguson.

Still looking for playmakers, the Sharks signed former Parramatta halfback Tim Smith and journey man hooker John Morris. Forward Adam Cuthbertson joined the club from Manly, while rookie fullback Nathan Gardner had a sensational debut season.

Cronulla began to put the horror season of 2009 behind them with a close 14-10 loss to premiers Melbourne in the opening round of the season.

The Sharks' defence crumbled with a 30-16 loss to the Warriors, and a 30-8 thrashing from Souths. The finally broke through for a win with an 11-0 victory over Parramatta in round four. The win ended an eleven game losing streak.

In round five, Cronulla were no match for Manly, conceding seven tries in a 40-12 loss. A 44-16 thumping from Brisbane the next week saw the Sharks fall to the bottom of the ladder.

Their time at the bottom was short lived, as Melbourne were sensationally stripped of all points due to a major salary cap scandal.

Winger Isaac Gordon scored two tries in a 26-6 win over Newcastle, but they were thrashed 38-0 by top of the table St George-Illawarra the following week.

Cronulla had the bye in round nine, but returned in the same form, going down 34-14 at home against Penrith. They upset Parramatta 22-18 before going down 20-4 to Brisbane. A surprise 42-18 thumping of Sydney Roosters in round thirteen saw the Sharks rise to thirteenth spot at the halfway mark of the season.

After another bye, Cronulla went down 22-4 to the Dragons before sneaking home 20-19 over North Queensland in golden point extra time. John Morris and Trent Barrett both kicked field goals in the match.

Cronulla lost 24-12 to an equally struggling Canterbury, and 21-10 to Newcastle, before again being thrashed by Manly, 48-18.

In round twenty, Cronulla were beaten 20-13 by Canberra, and only Melbourne's dramas prevented the Sharks from being in last place.

Ricky Stuart resigned as coach after the match, handing the reigns to Shane Flanagan. Stuart had announced his intention to step down as coach at the end of 2010 earlier in the year.

Cronulla started life under Flanagan with a 24-22 loss to Wests Tigers at Leichhardt. The next week they were comprehensively beaten 37-10 by the Warriors.

The Sharks upset Sydney Roosters 18-12 in round 23 to record their first win under their new coach. They were then beaten 24-4 by Melbourne, but bounced back to beat Gold Coast 30-16.

Cronulla finished the season on the wrong end of a 50-12 scoreline against second placed Penrith. The Sharks finished another miserable season in fourteenth place.

Nathan Gardner and Luke Covell finished in a tie as Cronulla's leading point scorer with 54 apiece. Gardner was also the club's top try scorer with eight, one ahead of Blake Ferguson and centre Dean Collis. Luke Covell announced his retirement at the end of the season after suffering a serious injury during the year.

2011

Veteran centre or winger Colin Best returned to Cronulla in 2011 after a stint with St George-Illawarra. He was joined by Dragons' teammate Jeremy Smith, and Penrith utility Wade Graham. Halfback Chad Townsend made his first grade debut during the 2011 season.

Things looked grim when Cronulla were belted by Canberra, 40-12, in the opening round. The Sharks recovered to upset premiers St George-Illawarra by 16-10 in round two.

In round three, five-eighth Albert Kelly scored two of Cronulla's seven tries as they thrashed Penrith 44-12. Winger John Williams kicked eight goals from eight attempts in the win.

The Sharks went down 26-18 to the Warriors and 19-13 to Manly. A 24-20 loss to Newcastle and a 30-12 defeat from North Queensland saw the Sharks in the familiar position of being near the bottom of the table after seven rounds.

Cronulla went down 31-12 to Souths before picking up two valuable points from a round nine bye. The week off did the Sharks some good, as they came back to beat 2010 runners up Sydney Roosters by 18-4.

The Sharks were belted 40-6 by Parramatta in round eleven, conceding seven tries. They then went down 14-8 to Melbourne and 34-16 to Brisbane to be in a three way tie for last place at the halfway mark of the competition.

After another bye, Cronulla defeated Canterbury 26-10. The next week they scored six tries on their way to a 36-12 away win over Gold Coast. Nathan Gardner, Paul Gallen, and winger Nathan Stapleton all crossed for two tries.

Two tries from Matthew Wright helped the Sharks to a 26-4 win over Souths, and when they beat Canberra 26-12 in round eighteen, Cronulla were on the cusp of the top eight.

The Sharks lost momentum when they were crushed 38-8 by St George-Illawarra; and an 18-0 loss to Newcastle saw their finals chances slip away.

In round 21, Cronulla let in eight tries, including a hat trick to Justin Hodges, as they were thrashed by Brisbane 46-16. A 20-16 loss to Gold Coast the next week officially ended any hopes of making the playoffs.

Cronulla lost 19-12 to Canterbury and 35-26 to Sydney Roosters. A 28-20 loss to North Queensland saw them in danger of finishing with the wooden spoon.

The Sharks ended their season with an eighth straight loss. They went down 30-22 to Wests Tigers, and finished in thirteenth spot, just one win ahead of last placed Gold Coast.

John Williams was Cronulla's top point scorer for the year with 76. Ben Pomeroy was their leading try scorer with nine, one ahead of Nathan Gardner.

2012

Cronulla lost their top two prop forwards at the end of 2011. Luke Douglas joined Gold Coast, while Kade Snowden returned to Newcastle. The club signed Wests Tigers pair Andrew Fifita and Bryce Gibbs to fill the gap, and also welcomed back hooker Isaac De Gois. The Sharks also gave a lifeline to troubled playmaker Todd Carney.

Cronulla started the season with a 17-16 loss to Wests Tigers in golden point extra time. They followed up with an 18-6 loss to Newcastle.

In round three, Cronulla produced a major upset by beating premiers Manly 17-14. Todd Carney's kicking proved the difference after both sides scored three tries.

Todd Carney was again the hero for Cronulla in their 20-14 away win over North Queensland. A 15-14 win over Penrith in round five, again thanks to the boot of Carney, saw Cronulla move into the top eight.

The Sharks moved up to fourth spot with a 12-0 win over St George-Illawarra, before beating Parramatta 24-18 and Canberra 44-22 to sit in third place. John Williams scored two of the Sharks' eight tries against the Raiders.

Cronulla went down 34-28 to Souths in round nine, but bounced back to beat the previously undefeated Melbourne by 12-10.

A 26-6 loss to Canterbury was followed by the bye round. The Sharks then went down 29-20 to Parramatta, to be in sixth place at the midway point of the season.

In round fourteen, Cronulla had a solid 22-12 win over Gold Coast. A 20-19 win over the Warriors the next week saw the Sharks in a four way tie for second spot, but fifth on percentages.

The Sharks moved into the top four with their second bye, and then beat Brisbane 26-12 at Lang Park. Veteran centre Colin Best scored two of their five tries.

Golden point extra time couldn't separate Cronulla and Sydney Roosters in round eighteen. Their tough 14-14 draw was enough to keep Cronulla in third spot.

The Sharks went down 18-10 to St George-Illawarra and 36-4 to Canberra to slip back to sixth place. In round 21, they went down 21-20 to Penrith in another golden point match.

Todd Carney scored two tries and 25 points in Cronulla's 45-4 thumping of the Warriors in Auckland in round 22. John Williams and Andrew Fifita also scored doubles.

The Sharks went down 26-4 to Newcastle, before beating Souths 20-7. Despite a 20-18 loss to Melbourne, Cronulla's place in the finals was secure; but they went into the playoffs without momentum after going down 36-22 to North Queensland in the last round of the regular season.

Cronulla's season came to an end when they conceded seven tries in a 34-16 loss to Canberra in the first week of the finals.

Todd Carney was Cronulla's top point scorer for the season with 141. Ben Pomeroy was their leading try scorer with nine, one ahead of Colin Best.

Despite making the finals for the first time since 2008, there were troubled times ahead for Cronulla.

2013

Cronulla signed goal kicking fullback Michael Gordon from Penrith for the 2013 season. Winger Beau Ryan and back rower Chris Heighington joined the club from Wests Tigers, as did veteran Penrith utility player Luke Lewis.

Chad Townsend returned to the club after a stint with the Warriors, and battled with Jeff Robson for the halfback role. The strong recruitment drive had Sharks fans thinking they could go deeper into the finals in 2013.

Before a ball was kicked, Cronulla's season descended into turmoil. They were named in the Australian Crime Commission's report on Drugs in Sport, and an investigation began. Several unnamed Sharks players were offered a six month ban, but all declined, as the club strenuously denied any wrong doing.

Shane Flanagan was stood down as head coach, and replaced by former Northern Eagles mentor Peter Sharp. He guided the Sharks to a 12-10 win over Gold Coast in the season opener.

Cronulla Chairman Daniel Irvine quit his role after the first round. The Sharks went down 14-12 to Souths before beating the Warriors 28-4, scoring five tries to one. After three rounds, Shane Flanagan returned to the coaching position.

The Sharks went down 25-12 to St George-Illawarra in round four, and then were beaten 13-6 by Parramatta, 25-18 by Manly and 24-8 by Canterbury. In the background, the investigation continued, and players were interviewed by the Australian Sports Anti-Doping Authority.

Back on the field, a field goal from Jeff Robson gave Cronulla a 21-20 golden point win over Newcastle in round eight.

The next week, winger Sosaia Feki scored two tries in the Sharks' 30-6 belting of Wests Tigers. The win saw Cronulla grab a share of eighth spot, despite the turmoil surrounding the club.

A 30-20 win over Canberra and a 14-12 win over Souths saw the Sharks enter the top eight. After a round twelve bye, the Sharks were smashed 38-6 by Melbourne, but were sixth at the halfway mark.

Jeff Robson scored two of Cronulla's five tries in their 32-14 win over Parramatta in round fourteen. After another bye, the Sharks went down 24-4 to North Queensland, but stayed in sixth place.

A 36-22 win over Wests Tigers, built on two tries from Andrew Fifita, was followed by a 19-18 away win over Brisbane, with Todd Carney kicking the crucial field goal.

In round nineteen, Cronulla were stunned by a 40-0 loss to Sydney Roosters. They bounced back to beat Penrith 38-10, with Todd Carney scoring eighteen points.

An 18-14 win over the Warriors was followed by a loss to Newcastle by the same scoreline. The Sharks' spot in the finals became safer with a 22-18 win over St George-Illawarra, and they confirmed their place with a 32-22 win over the Roosters in an amazing form reversal.

Cronulla went down 31-18 to North Queensland before finishing the regular season with a 38-18 away win over Canberra to wrap up fifth spot.

The Sharks won a controversial finals match against North Queensland 20-18, scoring four tries to three. They were involved in another controversial match the next week, going down 24-18 to Manly after a dubious try to Kieran Foran.

The loss ended Cronulla's season. That they made the second week of the finals was a testament to their ability to cope with the off field dramas, and Shane Flanagan's role in keeping the side together.

Towards the end of the year, ASADA finalised their report, but it was not made public. The NRL handed down a massive fine to the club, and suspended Shane Flanagan for the 2014 season. Peter Sharp again stepped into the role.

The saga continued into the 2014 season, as nine players were handed back dated suspensions. The players continued to deny any knowledge of taking any banned substances, and took the bans to end the drama surrounding the club. The bans had no impact on Cronulla's season, as they were imposed just before the finals.

It was an ugly period for Cronulla and rugby league in general, and showed the importance of the role of trainers and club doctors in trying to get the best out of players.

Michael Gordon was Cronulla's top point scorer in 2013 with 112, ahead of Todd Carney on 99. Andrew Fifita was the club's leading try scorer with nine, one ahead of Gordon.

2014

Centres Ben Pomeroy and Colin Best retired at the end of 2013. Ricky Leutele filled the gap after being on the verge of first grade for three seasons.

The club signed centre Blake Ayshford from Wests Tigers for extra depth, and also snared St George-Illawarra forward Matt Prior. Hooker Michael Lichaa and utility back Valentine Holmes made their debuts during the season.

Cronulla started the season with an 18-12 home loss to Gold Coast. In round two, they conceded seven tries in a 42-4 shellacking at the hands of Canterbury.

The Sharks went down 14-12 to St George-Illawarra and 30-0 to Newcastle, to be the only club without a win at the end of round four.

Cronulla broke through for their first win of the year when they beat the Warriors 37-6 in round five. Winger Nathan Stapleton scored four tries in the win.

The Sharks then went down 24-4 to 2013 runners up Manly, and 24-18 to premiers Sydney Roosters to remain in last spot.

Cronulla snuck home 24-20 against Penrith, before being hammered 42-24 by Parramatta, conceding eight tries.

The Sharks went down 22-20 to Wests Tigers and 18-0 to Souths before picking up two points from the bye. A 30-0 thumping from St George-Illawarra saw Cronulla still sitting in last place at the halfway mark of the season.

The Sharks moved ahead of Newcastle after their second bye, but were joined by the Knights in last place after going down 26-0 against Manly in round fifteen. It was the third match in a row that Cronulla had failed to score a point.

In a stunning upset, Cronulla beat Brisbane 24-22 at Lang Park, thanks to the faultless goal kicking of Michael Gordon. Shortly afterwards, Todd Carney was sacked from the club after an off-field incident.

The Sharks followed up with a 30-28 win over defending premiers Sydney Roosters, with the boot of Gordon again proving the difference.

The Sharks went down 31-18 to Newcastle and by 36-18 to North Queensland, before beating Penrith 18-16 in round twenty. They remained in last spot.

Cronulla lost 32-12 to Parramatta, and 16-12 to the Warriors, before suffering a 48-6 thrashing at the hands of Melbourne.

A 22-12 loss to fellow strugglers Canberra in round 24 saw the Sharks in outright last spot with just two rounds to play.

Cronulla were unlucky to gown 20-19 to North Queensland in golden point, and ended their season with a 26-10 loss to Wests Tigers. The Sharks finished with the wooden spoon for the first time since 1969.

Michael Gordon was the club's top point scorer with 124. Winger Sosaia Feki was Cronulla's leading try scorer with nine.

At the end of the season Shane Flanagan returned to the coaching role after serving his suspension. Peter Sharp had resigned from the position towards the end of the season, with James Shepherd temporarily filling the role.

2015

When Shane Flanagan returned to the coaching position, he was determined to build the club into a premiership force after two season of drama fuelled interruptions.

Veteran hooker Michael Ennis joined the club from Canterbury in a straight swap for Michael Lichaa. Centre Gerard Beale and utility back Ben Barba also signed with the Sharks, while rookie Jack Bird had a debut season to remember.

Cronulla showed plenty of commitment, but came up short in their opening match against Canberra, going down 24-20.

The Sharks went down 10-2 to Brisbane, 36-18 to Melbourne, and 24-22 to Gold Coast to find themselves in the familiar position of last place on the competition ladder.

A 20-12 win over Sydney Roosters eased the pressure. Jack Bird, playing five-eighth, scored two tries in the win.

Cronulla scored four tries to one in a 22-6 win over Newcastle to move away from the bottom of the table. They followed up with an 18-10 win over 2014 premiers South Sydney.

The Sharks went down 26-18 to Penrith, and 20-16 to the Warriors, before beating Gold Coast 23-22 in golden point. Winger Valentine Holmes kicked the winning field goal.

After a round eleven bye, Cronulla were smashed 42-6 by St George-Illawarra. A 10-4 win over the Roosters the following week saw the Sharks in twelfth spot at the midway point of the season.

Another bye and a 30-28 win over Newcastle had Cronulla on the cusp of the top eight at the end of round fifteen. Jack Bird scored a double against the Knights.

Cronulla upset North Queensland on their own turf, 24-18, but then went down 28-16 to a desperate Manly side, to squander an opportunity to move into the top eight.

A five tries to two 28-8 win over St George-Illawarra, and a 21-20 golden point win over Canberra saw Cronulla climb into eighth spot. Valentine Holmes was again the hero, kicking the decisive field goal against the Raiders.

In round twenty, Cronulla snuck home 18-16 against Canterbury. They beat the Warriors 18-14 in Auckland, and North Queensland 30-18 to move up to fifth spot.

Cronulla were soundly beaten 30-2 by Melbourne, before scoring seven tries to three in a 40-18 win over Wests Tigers. Valentine Holmes scored a double against the Tigers.

The Sharks moved into the top four with an exciting 35-28 win over Parramatta. Sosaia Feki scored two of their six tries. Cronulla went down 14-12 to Manly in an anti-climactic finish to the regular season, and ended up in sixth place.

Cronulla faced defending premiers South Sydney in the first week of the finals. The Sharks were too strong in the first half, with Jack Bird, Wade Graham and Anthony Tupou all scoring tries as they raced to an 18-0 lead at halftime. The Rabbitohs briefly rallied, but Cronulla hung on to win 28-12.

The Sharks saved their worst performance of the season for last. They conceded seven tries in an astonishing 39-0 defeat at the hands of North Queensland in their semi-final. The Cowboys would go on to win the competition for the first time, while Cronulla again lamented what could have been.

Michael Gordon was again Cronulla's leading point scorer with 164, ahead of Valentine Holmes on 89. Holmes was also the club's top try scorer with sixteen.

2016

Cronulla farewelled goal kicking fullback Michael Gordon at the end of the 2015 season. The former Penrith player signed with Parramatta. The club kept the rest of their main squad, and added Sydney Roosters premiership winning five-eighth James Maloney.

The Sharks kicked off their campaign with a 20-14 loss to 2015 premiers North Queensland. In round two, they scored five tries in a comprehensive 30-2 win over St George-Illawarra to get their season on track.

A 22-12 loss to Manly was followed by a hard fought 14-6 home win over Melbourne. When Cronulla beat Wests Tigers 34-26, thanks to eighteen points from James Maloney, they broke into the top eight.

Cronulla scored five tries to three in a 25-20 win over Gold Coast, and moved up to third spot after smashing Canberra 40-16 in round seven. Ben Barba scored a double against the Raiders.

The Sharks snuck home 20-18 against Penrith, despite the Panthers scoring four tries to three. The next week, Sosaia Feki scored two of Cronulla's five tries as they defeated Brisbane 30-28.

In round ten, Cronulla were at their attacking best. They ran in eleven tries, including four to Valentine Holmes and three to Sosaia Feki, as they equalled their biggest ever winning margin in a 62-0 annihilation of last placed Newcastle.

A tough 20-12 win over Manly was followed by a week off with the bye. The Sharks beat Canterbury 20-18 in round thirteen to be on top of the table at the halfway mark of the season.

Cronulla snuck home 13-10 against North Queensland, but fell to second spot on percentages after Melbourne belted Sydney Roosters 46-0.

After a second bye round, Cronulla defeated the Warriors 19-18 in golden point, thanks to a field goal from James Maloney. The win saw the Sharks return to the top of the table.

Two tries each from Sosaia Feki, Ricky Leutele and Gerard Beale helped Cronulla to a 34-24 win over Parramatta in round seventeen. A double from Ben Barba in a 26-10 win over Penrith ensured the Sharks remained on top of the table.

Sosaia Feki scored two of the Sharks' six tries in a 32-20 win over Sydney Roosters, and they followed by with an eight tries to one 36-4 rout of Newcastle. It was their fifteenth consecutive victory; the longest in the club's history.

In round 21, the winning streak came to an end when Cronulla were held to an 18-18 draw by Gold Coast, after they couldn't be separated by golden point extra time.

The Sharks went down 30-14 to Canberra, and lost their spot at the top of the table to Melbourne. Cronulla went down 32-18 to St George-Illawarra, and 12-6 to Souths, and fans were left wondering if their side had peaked too soon.

Cronulla found form in the second last round, running in six tries in a 37-12 win over Sydney Roosters. They ended the regular season with a heavy 26-6 loss to minor premiers Melbourne, and finished in third place.

In the opening round of the finals, Cronulla ended Canberra's ten match winning streak when five-eighth James Maloney kicked a late penalty goal to secure a 16-14 victory.

Cronulla enjoyed a week off, before facing defending premiers North Queensland in a Grand Final qualifier. The corresponding match had not been kind to the Sharks in the past, but they started well, forcing the Cowboys into uncharacteristic mistakes.

Sosaia Feki scored the first try of the match, and when Chad Townsend crossed, the Sharks had an unlikely 14-0 lead that took into the halftime break.

Lachlan Coote narrowed the gap with a try shortly after the interval, but Cronulla stormed home with tries to Luke Lewis, and two to James Maloney setting up a 32-6 lead. The Sharks relaxed to let the Cowboys score three consolation tries, but the comfortable 32-20 win propelled them into their first Grand Final since the 1997 Super League competition, and their first in a united competition since 1978.

James Maloney opened the scoring in the Grand Final with a penalty goal. Ben Barba scored a try from a scrum base set piece, and Cronulla found themselves up 8-0 at half time.

Melbourne hit back with tries to Will Chambers and Jesse Bromwich to take a 12-8 lead, and it seemed their experience in big matches would prove too much for the Sharks.

Prop forward Andrew Fifita had other ideas, and scored a barnstorming try to put Cronulla back in front 14-12.

Cronulla repelled the Melbourne attack in the final minutes to hang on to their slender lead, and claim the premiership for the first time in the club's history.

Cronulla's team that day was Ben Barba, Sosaia Feki, Jack Bird, Ricky Luetele, Valentine Holmes, James Maloney, Chad Townsend, Paul Gallen (capt), Wade Graham, Luke Lewis, Matt Prior, Michael Ennis and Andrew Fifita. The interchange players were Sam Tagataese, Chris Heighington, Gerard Beale and Jayson Bukuya. The coach was Shane Flanagan.

Luke Lewis was awarded the Clive Churchill Medal for being the best player on the ground, although Andrew Fifita and James Maloney had strong claims.

The premiership win was a triumph for Shane Flanagan, who had stuck solid with his squad during the 2013 drugs investigation; even enduring a season on the sidelines.

James Maloney was Cronulla's top point scorer with 219. Valentine Holmes was their leading try scorer with nineteen, three ahead of Ben Barba.

2017

Michael Ennis retired after the Grand Final victory. Ennis had played more than 270 first grade games since making his debut for Newcastle in 2003.

Cronulla kept the rest of their premiership winning squad with the exception of Ben Barba, who was granted a release following an off field incident. Barba later played for St Helens in England.

The Sharks began their premiership defence with a 26-18 loss to Brisbane. In round two, they smashed Canberra 42-16, with Wade Graham scoring three of their seven tries.

Cronulla went down 16-10 to St George-Illawarra, before beating Parramatta 20-6, and Newcastle by 19-18. James Maloney kicked the winning field goal against the Knights.

The Sharks beat Melbourne 11-2 in their first clash since the 2016 Grand Final. Cronulla then thumped Penrith 28-2, but went down 16-12 to Gold Coast in a major upset in round eight.

Cronulla bounced back to beat Wests Tigers 22-16, St George-Illawarra 18-14, North Queensland 18-14, and Canterbury 9-8 before enjoying a bye week. At the halfway mark of the season, Cronulla were in second place, a win behind Melbourne.

Round fourteen saw a top of the table clash between Melbourne and Cronulla. The Storm finished on top 18-13 to extend their lead as competition leader.

Cronulla edged out Wests Tigers 24-22, before copping a 35-18 loss to Manly which saw them drop out of the top four. The Sharks responded by smashing Sydney Roosters 44-12 to move back up to second spot.

After a second bye round, Cronulla were belted 30-10 by Gold Coast. They then defeated Souths 26-12 and the Warriors 26-12 to be in third place with five rounds to play.

Cronulla went down 30-12 to Canberra, and 32-10 to Brisbane, but retained their spot in the top four. In round 24, they beat North Queensland 26-16.

The Sharks dropped to fifth spot after a 16-14 loss to Sydney Roosters. In the final round, Cronulla beat Newcastle 26-18, but had to settle for fifth.

In the first week of the finals, Cronulla faced North Queensland. The premiership defence came to an end with a heartbreaking 17-16 loss.

Sosaia Feki was Cronulla's leading try scorer for the season with thirteen. Their top point scorer was James Maloney with 161.

2018

James Maloney joined Penrith for the 2018 season in a swap for the Panthers' Matt Moylan. Jack Bird left for Brisbane, and Chris Heighington had a final season with Newcastle.

Former test back Josh Dugan arrived from St George-Illawarra, and along with Moylan was the key recruit for the 2018 season.

Cronulla went down 20-14 to North Queensland in the opening round. They followed up with a 20-16 loss to St George-Illawarra, but registered a 14-4 win over Parramatta in round three.

The Sharks beat arch rival Melbourne 14-4, thanks to five goals from half Chad Townsend. They then went down 28-10 to Sydney Roosters, and 40-20 to St George-Illawarra to be in thirteenth place.

Jesse Ramien scored two tries in a 26-22 win over Penrith. Cronulla then snuck home 10-9 against Gold Coast, thanks to two field goals from Chad Townsend. A 22-20 win over Parramatta in round nine saw Cronulla move into the top eight.

Valentine Holmes notched a double in a 24-16 win over Canberra. The Sharks then beat Canterbury 22-16, and thumped Newcastle 48-10 on the back of three more tries from Holmes.

At the halfway mark of the season, Cronulla were in fourth spot. They went down 22-14 to Souths and fell to seventh place, but defeated Wests Tigers by 24-16 to stay in touch.

The Sharks went down 20-16 to Brisbane, before grafting an 18-15 away win against the Warriors. In round seventeen, the Sharks picked up two points from a bye, but were still a win short of fourth spot.

Valentine Holmes scored another two tries in a 24-12 win over Penrith. Cronulla beat Canberra 28-24, but a 12-10 loss to Brisbane hampered their efforts to move into the top four.

In round 21, Cronulla went down 33-32 to Manly in golden point extra time, thanks to a field goal from halfback Daly Cherry-Evans. The loss left the Sharks in sixth place with four rounds to play.

Cronulla rallied to upset Melbourne 17-14, before beating North Queensland 28-16. A 38-12 win over Newcastle saw Cronulla back in fourth spot. Edrick Lee scored two tries against the Knights.

Sosaia Feki notched a double in a 30-18 win over Canterbury in the final round. Cronulla hung to fourth spot in a tight finish which saw the top four finish on an equal number of points.

In the first week of the finals, Cronulla faced minor premiers Sydney Roosters. The Sharks went down 21-12, making every game a must win.

Cronulla snuck home 21-20 against Penrith, courtesy of a Chad Townsend field goal; but couldn't overcome Melbourne, going down 22-6 in the Grand Final qualifier.

Valentine Holmes was easily Cronulla's leading try scorer for the season with 22. Chad Townsend was the Sharks' top point scorer for the year with 148; his four field goals edging him ahead of Holmes, who finished on 144.

During the off-season, Shane Flanagan was deregistered as a coach by the NRL following evidence of him breaking the conditions of his previous suspension. Former utility player and National Youth Competition coach John Morris was appointed head coach for the 2019 season.

2019

Valentine Holmes shocked Cronulla and the rugby league community during the off-season, when he opted to try his luck in America's National Football League. The Sharks also lost key backs Edrick Lee and Jesse Ramien to Newcastle, while forward Luke Lewis announced his retirement after playing over 320 first grade games, including 116 for Cronulla.

The Sharks signed Canterbury centre Josh Morris, and Warriors' halfback Shaun Johnson; and unearthed an exciting centre in Bronson Xerri.

Cronulla's season began with a 14-8 loss to Newcastle. They recovered to beat Gold Coast 20-6 before thumping North Queensland 42-16. Josh Morris and Chad Townsend each scored two tries against the Cowboys.

Cronulla went down 24-12 to Parramatta, and by 30-16 to defending premiers Sydney Roosters, before beating Penrith 24-20. A 29-6 loss to Brisbane saw the Sharks in ninth place after seven rounds.

The Sharks upset Melbourne 20-18 to move back into the top eight; and followed up with a 26-18 win over Gold Coast. Josh Morris and Aaron Gray each scored two tries against the Titans.

Cronulla again fell out of the top eight following a 24-14 loss to Manly in round ten. The following week, Bronson Xerri scored three tries in a 22-9 win over St George-Illawarra. Cronulla then enjoyed a bye week before smashing Parramatta 42-22 to be in sixth place at the midway point of the season. Bronson Xerri notched a double against the Eels.

The Sharks were pipped 22-20 by Canberra, 14-12 bt Canterbury, and 24-22 by Brisbane. The trio of close losses saw Cronulla slip to eighth place, ahead of Wests Tigers and Penrith on percentages.

After being hammered 40-16 by Melbourne, and losing their spot in the top eight, Cronulla went down 19-18 to the Warriors. They kept their season alive with a 16-14 win over North Queensland, and a 39-24 victory over Souths. Bronson Xerri scored another two tries against the Rabbitohs, as the Sharks climbed to seventh place.

Cronulla lost 26-20 to Penrith, before beating St George-Illawarra 18-12 to stay in the top eight. In round 23, Josh Morris bagged a double as Cronulla belted the Warriors 42-16.

The following week, Cronulla went down 15-14 to Canberra in golden point extra time. They secured their spot in the finals with a 25-8 win over Wests Tigers in the final round.

Cronulla finished in seventh place, and faced Manly in the first week of the finals. They lost 28-16 to end a frustrating season.

Josh Morris proved to be an astute signing, as he finished the year as Cronulla's leading try scorer with fifteen; two ahead of Bronson Xerri. Shaun Johnson was the Sharks' top point scorer for the season with 102.

2020

The 2020 season was like no other. The outbreak of the COVID-19 pandemic saw the season suspended for two months after just two rounds. Teams were forced to live in safety bubbles in order to keep the season alive. The competition was reduced to twenty rounds.

Cronulla blooded a number of newcomers to first grade, including backs Sione Katoa, Ronaldo Mulitalo and William Kennedy; and forwards Toby Rudolf and Blayke Brailey. They welcomed Jesse Ramien back to the club, but were rocked by the suspension of Bronson Xerri for allegedly using performance enhancing substances. Xerri was later suspended for four years.

Paul Gallen announced his retirement after 348 games in nineteen seasons. A veteran of 32 tests for Australia, Gallen has since embarked on a successful boxing career.

Cronulla went down 22-18 to Souths in the opening round, and followed up with a 12-10 loss to Melbourne. When the competition resumed, the Sharks lost 28-16 to Wests Tigers, before opening their account with a 26-16 win over North Queensland. Jesse Ramien and Ronald Mulitalo both scored two tries against the Cowboys, who featured former Shark Valentine Holmes in their squad after his return from a sojourn in the NFL.

The Sharks went down 30-16 to St George-Illawarra before beating Canterbury 20-18, thanks to three tries from winger Sione Katoa.

Cronulla defeated Manly 40-22, and thumped Gold Coast 40-10 to move into the top eight after eight rounds. The Sharks were smashed 56-24 by Penrith, before thrashing the Warriors 46-10 on the back of doubles from Sione Katoa and Jesse Ramien. At the midway point of the season, Cronulla sat in ninth place, just outside of the top eight on percentages.

Cronulla moved back into the top eight with a 28-24 win over St George-Illawarra. They consolidated their spot with a 36-26 win over Brisbane, off-setting a 14-12 loss to Parramatta.

The Sharks beat Gold Coast 30-18, before copping a 38-12 belting from Penrith. With five rounds to go, Cronulla were in eighth place.

Cronulla defeated North Queensland 28-12, but a 38-10 thumping from Newcastle saw them remain vulnerable in the race for the finals. The Sharks wrapped up their spot when two tries from Ronaldo Mulitalo helped them to a 22-14 win against the Warriors.

Cronulla went down 34-18 to Sydney Roosters before ending the regular season with a 38-28 loss to Canberra. The Sharks finished in eighth spot.

In the first week of the finals, Cronulla's season came to an end with a 32-20 loss to Canberra. Sione Katoa was the club's top try scorer for the season with sixteen. Their leading point scorer for the year was Shaun Johnson with 120.

2021

The 2021 season was again battered by COVID-19, but the competition went ahead as planned. Clubs were again forced to play and train in safety bubbles, and the entire league was moved to Queensland towards the end of the season.

Cronulla began their campaign with a 32-18 win over St George-Illawarra. Fullback William Kennedy scored two tries against the Dragons.

The Sharks went down 12-10 to Canberra, and 28-4 to Parramatta before belting North Queensland by 48-10. William Kennedy and Connor Tracey both notched doubles against the Cowboys.

After going down 25-18 to Sydney Roosters, Cronulla decided to replace John Morris as coach with Josh Hannay. The Sharks announced Craig Fitzgibbon would be head coach in 2022.

Cronulla lost 26-22 to Newcastle, and 18-12 to Canterbury before being thrashed 40-14 by defending premiers Melbourne. After eight rounds the Sharks were in thirteenth place.

Cronulla were ambushed 48-0 by Penrith, and then went down 32-22 to Souths. In round eleven, they snuck home 13-12 against St George-Illawarra, thanks to a field goal from Chad Townsend.

Ronaldo Mulitalo scored two tries in a 38-10 victory over Gold Coast which left Cronulla in twelfth spot, but within a win of the top eight, at the halfway mark of the competition.

After a bye round, Cronulla upset Penrith 19-18. Shaun Johnson kicked the winning field goal. The Sharks then snuck home 26-24 against North Queensland, and crept into the top eight.

Cronulla kept eighth spot despite a 26-18 loss to Brisbane. They bounced back to beat the Warriors 20-12, before going down 34-18 to Canberra.

In round nineteen, Sione Katoa scored two tries in a 44-24 win over Canterbury. Cronulla went down 40-22 to Manly, and 18-16 to the Warriors to slip out of the top eight with four rounds to play.

After a tight 16-14 loss to Newcastle, Cronulla crushed Wests Tigers 50-20 to move back up to eighth place. Cronulla beat Brisbane 24-16, but missed out on a finals spot when they went down 28-16 to Melbourne in the final round.

The Sharks finished in ninth spot, behind Gold Coast on for and against. William Kennedy and Connor Tracey were the top try scorers for the year with fourteen each. Young utility back Braydon Trindall was the club's leading point scorer with 88.

2022

Cronulla had a new coach for the 2022 season. Former test forward Craig Fitzgibbon took on the role after years in the Sydney Roosters system. Fitzgibbon's father Alan had coached the Sharks during a successful period in the late 1980s.

Cronulla recruited well, signing premiership winning forward Dale Finucane from Melbiurne, as well as his team mate, rookie utility back Nicho Hynes. Shaun Johnson returned to the NZ Warriors, while Josh Dugan announced his retirement before playing in NSW country.

The Sharks were unlucky to go down 24-19 to Canberra in the opening round after the Raiders scored a late try. They recovered to sneak home 18-16 against Parramatta, before smashing St George-Illawarra 36-12 at Wollongong.

Cronulla beat Newcastle 18-0, before belting Wests Tigers 30-4 on the back of two tries from Sione Katoa. The Sharks then went down 34-18 to Melbourne, and sat in third place after six rounds.

Ronaldo Mulitalo and Siosifa Talakai each scored two tries as Cronulla beat Manly 34-22. The Sharks then went down 16-7 to Brisbane in an upset, but remained in the top four.

Utility back Connor Tracey scored two tries as Cronulla beat NZ Warriors 29-10. The Sharks briefly fell out of the top four with a 30-10 loss to Canberra, but bounced back to beat Gold Coast by 25-18. However, the Sharks 36-16 loss to Sydney Roosters in round twelve to sit in seventh place at the halfway mark of the season.

After a bye round, Cronulla defeated NZ Warriors 38-16. Sione Katoa scored three tries in the win which saw Cronulla move back into fifth place.

Cronulla defeated Gold Coast 18-10 and Canterbury 18-6 before upsetting Melbourne 28-6 to move back into the top four. Jesse Ramien scored three tries against the Storm.

Ramien crossed for a double in a 26-12 away win over North Queensland in round eighteen. The Sharks went down 20-10 to Penrith before sneaking home 21-20 against Souths in golden point extra time thanks to a field goal from Nicho Hynes.

The Sharks beat St George-Illawarra 24-18, Wests Tigers 36-12 and Manly 40-6 to secure their place in the top four. Nicho Hynes bagged twenty points against the Sea Eagles.

After shutting out Canterbury 16-0, Cronulla beat Newcastle 38-16 on the back of three tries from

Briton Nikora, and finished the season in second place, two wins behind Penrith.

In the first week of the finals, Cronulla hosted North Queensland. The match saw the lead change several times before it finished in a 30-30 draw. William Kennedy scored two tries for the Sharks. In golden point extra time, former Cronulla player Valentine Holmes kicked a two point field goal to give the Cowboys a 32-30 victory.

Cronulla faced Souths the following week, but were no match for the Rabbitohs, going down 38-12 to end their season. A disappointing finals campaign ended a positive season for Cronulla, whose rookie coach looked like being a long term success.

Winger Ronaldo Mulitalo was Cronulla's top try scorer for the season with seventeen. Their leading point scorer was Nicho Hynes with 194.

2023

Cronulla were looking to build on their successful 2022 by progressing further in the finals. Long serving prop and 2016 Grand Final hero Andrew Fifita had retired, but the Sharks retained the rest of their 2022 squad.

In the opening round, Cronulla went down 27-18 to Souths. They recovered to beat Parramatta 30-26 on the back of three tries from William Kennedy. The Sharks then went down 24-20 to Canberra, before smashing St George-Illawarra 40-8. The form guide in the opening month made it hard to gauge Cronulla's chances of winning the title. Ronaldo Mulitalo and Jesse Ramien each scored two tries against the Dragons.

The Sharks were pipped 32-30 by New Zealand Warriors, before picking up two points from a bye round. After their rest, Cronulla defeated Sydney Roosters 22-12 to move into the top eight at the end of round seven.

Fullback William Kennedy bagged another hat trick in a 33-20 victory over Canterbury; and a 44-6 demolition of North Queensland saw Cronulla in the top four. Ronaldo Mulitalo scored two of the Sharks' seven tries against the Cowboys.

A 36-16 loss to the new Brisbane based Dolphins franchise was followed by a rare 20-14 win over Manly at Brookvale Oval. Cronulla beat Newcastle 26-6 in Coffs Harbour, and another bye round saw them grab a share of the competition lead alongside Penrith, Brisbane and Melbourne.

Cronulla lost their spot at the top of the ladder with a 20-12 home loss to Brisbane in a top of the table clash. The following week, they were hammered 54-10 by Melbourne, and doubts about their ability to compete with the top teams resurfaced.

In round 16, Cronulla scored eight tries in a 48-10 thumping of struggling Canterbury. After another bye round, they thrashed St George-Illawarra by 52-16, with Ronaldo Mulitalo and Briton Nikora each scoring two of the Sharks' nine tries.

Winger Sione Katoa scored three tries, and centre Siosifa Talakai bagged a double as Cronulla defeated Wests Tigers 36-12 to retain their spot in the top four after nineteen rounds. However, the Sharks were no match for New Zealand Warriors the next week, going down 44-12 in Auckland. A 30-26 upset loss to Manly in round 21 saw Cronulla fall to sixth place.

The 28-0 loss to Penrith in round 22 saw pundits begin to wonder if Cronulla could progress if they qualified for the finals. Big losses to Penrith, New Zealand Warriors and Melbourne placed a question mark over their premiership credentials.

Two tries from five-eighth Braydon Trindall set up a 26-16 victory over Souths in Perth; and a 36-6 thumping of Gold Coast saw Cronulla still a chance of finishing in the top four. Ronaldo Mulitalo notched another double against the Titans.

After recording a 32-12 away win over North Queensland, the Sharks were smashed 32-6 by Newcastle, ending their top four chances. In the final round, Cronulla defeated Canberra 24-6, and finished in sixth place.

In the first week of the finals, Cronulla faced Sydney Roosters, who had snuck into the finals after a last round win over Souths. A tough match was only decided by a field goal from Sam Walker, giving Sydney Roosters a 13-12 victory. It was another disappointing season end for the Sharks.

Ronaldo Mulitalo was Cronulla's leading try scorer for the season with 21. Their top point scorer was Nicho Hynes with 187.

TOP POINT SCORERS

Steve Rogers 1255
Mat Rogers 1112
Luke Covell 948
Andrew Ettingshausen 662
Barry Andrews 657
Alan Wilson 516
Brett Kimmorley 467
David Peachey 440
Mitch Healey 418
Chad Townsend 402
Michael Gordon 400
Terry Hughes 388
Nicho Hynes 381
James Maloney 380
Valentine Holmes 369
Dean Carney 286
Sosaia Feki 268
Shaun Johnson 263
Ronaldo Mulitalo 260
George Taylforth 259
Paul Gallen 257
Sean Watson 252
Todd Carney 249
Sione Katoa 238
Jonathan Docking 228
Colin Best 224
David Simmons 216

TOP TRY SCORERS

Andrew Ettingshausen 165
David Peachey 110
Steve Rogers 82
Mat Rogers 75
Sosaia Feki 67
Valentine Holmes 66
Ronaldo Mulitalo 65
Ray Corcoran 63
Paul Gallen 63
Sione Katoa 59
Jonathan Docking 57
Colin Best 56
Luke Covell 55
David Simmons 54
Ben Pomeroy 53
Mick Mullane 53
Adam Dykes 47
Jesse Ramien 45
Steve Edmonds 45
Dave Chamberlin 45
Chris Gardner 44
Paul Mellor 43
Glenn Coleman 41
Wade Graham 41

MOST MATCHES

Paul Gallen 348
Andrew Ettingshausen 327
Wade Graham 249
David Peachey 232
Mitch Healey 222
Dane Sorensen 216
Andrew Fifita 212
Danny Lee 212
Greg Pierce 210
Steve Rogers 202
David Hatch 186
Adam Dykes 183
Gavin Miller 180
Jayson Bukuya 168
Jason Stevens 167
Jonathan Docking 161
Dean Treister 161
Ben Pomeroy 158
Mark McGaw 157
Michael Porter 149
Sosaia Feki 148
Rick Bourke 146
Andrew Pierce 146
Chad Townsend 146
Craig Dimond 142
Brett Kimmorley 140
Nathan Long 139

Bibliography

Malcolm Andrews, "The ABC of Rugby League", Australian Broadcasting Corporation, 2006

Steve Haddan, "The Finals – 100 Years of National Rugby League Finals", Steven Haddan C/O QLD TV Limited, 2008

Alan Whiticker & Glen Hudson, "The Encyclopedia of Rugby League Players", Gary Allen Pty Ltd, 2007

Other material has come from a number of sources, including:

Big League

Rugby League Week

Sydney Morning Herald

The Daily Mirror, Sydney

The Daily Telegraph, Sydney

Some of the statistics have been obtained from www.rlstats.com

Printed in Great Britain
by Amazon

45099412R00099